ENCOURAGING
THE HEART

ENCOURAGING
THE HEART

A LEADER'S GUIDE TO REWARDING
AND RECOGNIZING OTHERS

James M. Kouzes
Barry Z. Posner

AUTHORS OF
THE LEADERSHIP CHALLENGE

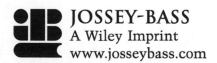

JOSSEY-BASS
A Wiley Imprint
www.josseybass.com

Published by Jossey-Bass
A Wiley Imprint
989 Market Street, San Francisco, CA 94103-1741   www.josseybass.com

Jossey-Bass books and products are available through most bookstores. To contact Jossey-Bass directly call our Customer Care Department within the U.S. at 800-956-7739, outside the U.S. at 317-572-3986 or fax 317-572-4002.

Jossey-Bass also publishes its books in a variety of electronic formats. Some content that appears in print may not be available in electronic books.

Library of Congress Cataloging-in-Publication Data
Kouzes, James M., 1945–
    Encouraging the heart : a leader's guide to rewarding and recognizing others / by James M. Kouzes and Barry Z. Posner.—1st pbk. ed.
        p.   cm.—(The Jossey-Bass business & management series)
    Includes bibliographical references and index.
    ISBN 0-7879-6463-8 (alk. paper)
    1. Leadership.   2. Executive ability.   3. Interpersonal relations.   4. Incentives in industry.   5. Performance awards.   6. Employee motivation.   I. Posner, Barry Z.   II. Title.   III. Series.
HD57.7 .K679   2003
658.4'092—dc21   2002152873

Printed in the United States of America
FIRST EDITION
HB Printing   10 9 8 7 6
PB Printing   10 9 8 7 6 5 4 3

The Jossey-Bass
Business & Management Series

CONTENTS

C ourage. Encourage. Two words, same origin. Heart. You gotta have heart. Miles and miles and miles of it. There's no bravery or boldness without heart. There's no spirit or support without heart. There's no sacrifice or soul without heart. Nothing great ever gets done without heart. You gotta have heart.

And at the heart of leadership is caring. Without caring, leadership has no purpose. And without showing others that you care and what you care about, other people won't care about what you say or what you know. As a relationship, leadership requires a connection between leaders and their constituents over matters, in the simplest sense, of the heart. It is personal and it is interpersonal.

We need heart because the struggle to the top is arduous. Our research tells us that if we're going to make it to the summit we *need* someone shouting in our ear, "Come on, you can do it. I know you can do it!" It's not something we easily admit—a lot of times we think we can do it alone. But we all really do need encouragement. Encouragement boosts performance, strengthens our resolve, and improves our health. Otherwise, why perform to an audience? Why not just sing to an empty room, play to an empty arena, or sell only to yourself? We need the applause and knowing that we're connecting to others in order to do our best. We need the enthusiasm and the energy from others.

We need to feel connected to others and, in turn, they to us, because greatness is never achieved all by ourselves—alone. Encouraging the Heart is the leadership practice that connects us with one another. It signals and documents that we're in "this" together—whatever this project, program, campaign, neighborhood, congregation, division, and so on, may be. Social capital joins financial and intellectual capital as the necessary ingredients for organizational success. In creating social capital leaders encourage the heart so that people will want to be with and for one another. When leaders commend individuals for achieving the values or goals of the organization, they give them courage, inspiring them to experience their own ability to deliver—even when the pressure is on. When we recognize women and men for their contributions we expand their awareness of their value to the organization and to their co-workers, imparting a sense of connectedness that, being social animals, all humans seek. While we may all be connected, leaders make sure that we're *in touch*.

Since discovering the importance of Encouraging the Heart more than two decades ago, and first writing this entire volume to enable others to more effectively engage in this key leadership practice, the world has changed. Yet the leadership practice of encouraging could not be any more timely or needed. Nothing on the horizon suggests, moreover, that its importance will diminish.

THE HEART OF THE MATTER

Encouraging the Heart is about the principles and practices that support the basic human need to be appreciated for who we are and what we do. It's about how leaders can apply these principles and practices to their daily work. This is not a book about glad-handing, back-slapping, gold stars, and pay-offs. It's about the importance of linking rewards and appreciation to standards of excellence. It about why encouragement is absolutely essential to sustaining people's commitment to organizations and outcomes. It's about the hard work it takes to get extraordinary things done in organizations, and it's about ways to enhance your own ability in—and comfort with—recognizing and celebrating the achievements of others.

Encouraging the Heart has its origins in our research on the practices of individuals when they were functioning at their *personal best as leaders.* Since our studies began more than two decades ago, we've collected thousands of best practice leadership case studies and analyzed tens of thousands of leadership assessment instruments. We've consistently found that when getting extraordinary things done, leaders:[1]

- Model the Way
- Inspire a Shared Vision
- Challenge the Process
- Enable Others to Act
- Encourage the Heart

All Five Practices® are essential to exemplary leadership. All contribute to explaining why leaders are successful. Each plays it own distinct part, and none alone is sufficient. So why have we written a book solely about only one practice, *Encouraging the Heart?* There are four reasons.

The first is practicality. We couldn't find sufficient resources on the bookshelves to share with our students and the practicing managers attending our classes and workshops. In other cases, we simply weren't very satisfied with what little there was. We wanted to offer a set of principles, practices, and examples that would provide leaders with a repeatable process—a set of essential actions—they could apply in their own settings.

The second reason is principle. For too long now, we've been hearing the human side of business referred to as the "soft" side, and encouraging the heart seems about as soft as you can get. In fact some of our clients have told us the phrase *encouraging the heart* wouldn't work in their cultures and asked if we could change the name of the practice. We never have, and we never will. In this book, we will not only demonstrate that encouraging the heart is not soft; we show how powerful a force it is in achieving high standards and stretch goals. If you're after results, then you'd better start paying attention to encouraging the heart.

Third, we were curious. In all the data we've gathered from thousands of leaders about the Five Practices of Exemplary Leadership®,[2] the only one of the five practices in which there may be a significant difference in how men and women see themselves is encouraging the heart. Can you guess who scores higher, who exhibits more encouragement: male or female leaders? If you guessed women—as most people do— you're correct, but only partially so. It's a bit more compli- cated. First, about as many studies have found a difference between males and females as those studies that have found no difference. Second, the responses of constituents tend to be much more gender-neutral. That is, female constituents do not report that their leaders encourage the heart any more than do male constituents, regardless of the gender of the leader. We've been intrigued for some time by this finding, and we wanted to explore the practice in depth to see if we could understand more about these differences. We also wanted to document that encouraging the heart is more related to being effective as a leader than it is about any gender-role stereo-typing.

The final reason we chose to write *Encouraging the Heart* is that we wanted to add our voices to the discussion of soul and spirit in the workplace. Leaders create relationships, and one of these relationships is between individuals and their work. Ultimately we all work for a purpose, and that common purpose has to be served if we are to feel encouraged. Encouraging the heart only works if there's a fit between the person, the work, and the organization.

To this final point, it is interesting to note that the word *encouragement* has its root in the Latin word *cor*, which literally means "heart." So does the word *courage*. To have courage means to have heart. To *en*courage—to provide with or give courage—literally means to give others heart. Richard I, king of England from 1189 to 1199, was glorified for his courage. How was he called by the troubadours? Richard the Lion-Hearted.

The heroic tradition from which this language comes tells us that when we're talking about courage and encouragement, we don't simply mean the sentimental notion that's expressed on contemporary greeting cards. Rather, in this context the word *heart* brings forth images of courage when faced with great challenges, hope when confronted with great difficulties, and the fortitude to reach inside and give your best even when faced with great odds. Heart involves strength and toughness. It involves leaders' awareness of their responsibilities to those they're entrusted to lead, as well as to the values of the organizations that select them. It involves a capacity to forcefully impart cherished values to the people who look to them for leadership.

But heart, *cor*, has a double meaning. From its root also comes the word "cordial." Encouragement is about being generous and charitable. It's about having a "big heart." When leaders encourage the heart of their constituents, they are also showing how profoundly grateful they are for the dedication and commitment others have shown to the cause.

Encouraging the heart, then, is about the dichotomous nature of leadership. It's about toughness and tenderness. Guts and grace. Firmness and fairness. Fortitude and gratitude. Passion and compassion. Leaders must have courage themselves, and they must impart it to others. This book is about how leaders effectively give of their hearts so that others may more fully develop and experience their own.

WHO SHOULD READ THIS BOOK?

As with our other books, *The Leadership Challenge* and *Credibility*, this one, too, is written to assist people in furthering their abilities to lead others in getting extraordinary things done. Whether you're in the public or private sector; whether you're an employee or volunteer; whether you're on the front lines or in the senior ranks; whether you're a student, a teacher, or a parent, we've written this book to help you develop your capacity to guide others to places they've never been before.

In this book, you find numerous examples of how ordinary people exercise leadership. These are folks just like the rest of us. What you don't find here are a bunch of examples about famous CEOs and celebrity leaders. It's not that they couldn't benefit from *Encouraging the Heart;* it's just that they represent such a small percentage of the people who lead that they don't dominate our view of what leadership is and what leaders do. Most likely you don't know, or haven't heard about, the people we report on, but we're certain you know people like them in your workplace.

To us, *leadership is everyone's business*. Leadership is not about a position or a place. It's an attitude and a sense of responsibility for making a difference. Even if you don't consider yourself to be in a leadership role now, you may find yourself in one soon. *Encouraging the Heart* can be helpful to you as you prepare for that eventuality. In our studies of people functioning at their personal bests as leaders, we've written about people as young as nine and older than eighty who have assumed leadership roles. So don't count yourself out.

It's been our experience that leaders most often want answers to questions that begin with *How do I . . . ?* So we'll offer many how-to's in this book. But it's also our intention to go beyond providing a prescriptive list of things to do. We want to offer you a set of principles that guide you in developing your own methods and techniques. That's where most of the fun is, anyway.

A LEADER'S GUIDE

We've subtitled this book "A Leader's Guide to Rewarding and Recognizing Others." *Encouraging the Heart* is designed to describe what leaders do, explain the principles underlying their practices, provide some examples of real leaders demonstrating these actions, and then offer suggestions on how you can get started putting them into practice.

The first three chapters introduce you to the basic message about encouraging the heart: the best leaders care. In Chapter One, we show you the research to support this point of view, and in Chapter Two we present a classic case study to illustrate the seven essentials of encouraging the heart. Once you learn to master each of these, you're well on your way to becoming a caring and credible leader. In Chapter Three, we offer an Encouragement Index, to assess the extent to which you think you exhibit each of the essentials.

Chapters Four through Ten explore the seven essentials in some detail. Although the discussions are built on our original and ongoing research, we expand our understanding of encouraging by drawing on the research of other scholars. We also illustrate each essential with case examples.

Chapter Four explains why encouraging the heart begins by being clear about standards. Unless there are clear values and principles, it's hit-or-miss when it comes to knowing what's right and the right things to do. It's also tough for the leader to know how to recognize performance when he or she doesn't know what to look for. Chapter Five is about the leader's attitude toward others. Expecting the best is the only way we get the best, and this chapter tells us why and how "Pygmalion leaders" make the best leaders.

When successful leaders expect the best, they're much more able to pay attention to what's going on around them and find examples of people who are living up to and exceeding expectations. As we see in Chapter Six, leaders are always on the lookout for exemplars of the values and standards. In Chapter Seven, we learn the power of personalizing recognition. The best leaders get to know the person. When it comes time to recognize, leaders know a way to make it special, meaningful, and memorable.

In Chapter Eight, we talk about how great leaders are great storytellers. Storytelling is one of humankind's oldest ways to communicate life's lessons, and leaders find ways to broadcast and publicize stories of recognition. People learn best from those they can most relate to, so leaders use all available media to brag about the good things going on in their organizations. In Chapter Nine, we see how leaders bring people together to share the successes of their colleagues and to provide needed support to each other. Social support is absolutely essential to our well-being and to our productivity.

We conclude our discussion of the seven essentials by reiterating one of our consistent messages: to be credible, leaders must do what they expect others to do. Chapter Ten is about how leaders set an example and create a climate for encouraging the heart. We sum it all up in Chapter Eleven and then leave you in Chapter Twelve with 150 ways to get started in your quest to encourage the hearts of your constituents.

In reading and applying the material in each of these chapters, we hope that you'll realize that encouraging the heart is much more than being nice to people or acting like a cheerleader. Encouraging the heart means employing a set of principles and practices that, taken as a whole, add up to a powerful force in mobilizing people.

KEEPING HOPE ALIVE

We're living in a time that holds great promise. New developments in pharmaceuticals and biotechnology promise that some of the most deadly and disabling diseases may be cured or at least better managed. New information technologies promise not only to connect us globally and to create whole new forms of commerce but also to foster peace and expand the reaches of our educational systems. Fledgling democratic movements promise to free people from centuries of tyranny and fear.

And at this same time in history, we're suffering from a severe hangover caused by the excesses of the late 1990s and early years of the new millennium. Corporate scandals seem to be a regular part of the nightly news, and we've come so far as to require CEOs to personally and explicitly sign-off on their corporate numbers. The horrific and fateful events of September 11, 2001, continue as part of the background of international tension, making few of us feel as personally safe as we once did. We're wondering when we're really going to hit bottom and if our lives will ever be the same again.

But what is a promise without hope—hope that these promises will be kept? Bold leadership is required if we are to keep hope alive, and *Encouraging the Heart* is ultimately about keeping hope alive. Leaders keep hope alive when they set high standards and genuinely express optimism about an individual's capacity to achieve them. They keep hope alive when they give feedback and publicly recognize a job well done. They keep hope alive when they give their constituents the internal support that all human beings need to feel that they and their work are important and have meaning. They keep hope alive when they train and coach people to exceed their current capacities. Most important, leaders keep hope alive when they set an example. There really is nothing more encouraging than to see our leaders practice what they preach.

These are tough times for many people, but the path to the future has always been full of challenges and opportunities. There's some apprehensiveness in our actions, a touch of cynicism in our attitudes, and a creeping weariness in our bodies. Deep down, however, you and I know we'll get through these times. We always have—with courage and encouragement.

ENCOURAGING

THE HEART

PART ONE

CHAPTER ONE

The Heart of Leadership

Really believe in your heart of hearts that your fundamental purpose, the reason for being, is to enlarge the lives of others. Your life will be enlarged also. And all of the other things we have been taught to concentrate on will take care of themselves.
—PETE THIGPEN, Executive Reserves

A sk yourself this question: Do I need encouragement to perform at my best?

We've asked our leadership classes, and at first the answers surprised us. We knew from our previous research that performance was higher when people were led by individuals who gave more encouragement,[1] so we naturally expected that almost everyone would answer yes.

We were wrong. Only about 60 percent reported that they needed encouragement to do their best. Puzzled, we asked them to tell us why.

They told us that they didn't *need* encouragement. They *could* do their best without it. The majority believed themselves to be individuals with lots of personal initiative and responsibility, and that needing encouragement implied they couldn't perform well unless someone was around to cheer them on and tell them they were doing a good job.

Their responses made us intensely curious. How could it be that performance was higher among leaders who were more encouraging of others, but almost half were telling us they didn't need it?

So we reframed the question: "When you get encouragement, does it help you perform at a higher level?" This time about 98 percent said yes, and only 2 percent said no. These responses are in line with a study by the training and development company Kepner-Tregoe, in which researchers found that 96 percent of the North American workers they studied agreed with the statement "I get a lot of satisfaction out of knowing I've done a good job."[2]

STARVED FOR RECOGNITION

So we get a lot of satisfaction from positive feedback, and encouragement helps if we get it. Why, then, do we *think* we don't need much positive affirmation?

Perhaps it's because we don't experience enough encouragement to realize how important it is. Most workers don't get much recognition for a job well done, and most managers don't give it, according to the Kepner-Tregoe study. Only about 40 percent of North American workers say they receive any recognition for a job well done, and about the same percentage report they *never* get recognized for outstanding individual performance.[3]

Think about this for a moment. You bust your butt to get that shipment out early, or make that customer feel really special, or invent a way to fix that troublesome glitch in the product, and you *never* get even a thank-you. Apparently, this happens to too many of us—or perhaps all of us at one time or another.

No wonder. Only 50 percent of managers say they give recognition for high-performance.[4] Evidently, most assume that getting extraordinary things done is just part of the job.

Paul Moran certainly felt this way at one time in his managerial career. "In the past," he explained, "I usually neglected to celebrate my team's accomplishments (and my own accomplishments) because I personally never placed much importance on this aspect of the job for myself, and I tended to forget about recognizing the accomplishments of others. Rather, I treated their accomplishments as part of their normal job, which required no unique recognition."[5]

When Moran went to work at Pacific Bell, however, he took another look at the importance he gave to recognizing others and celebrating successes. He found, in fact, that it did make a difference to others, so he decided to change his leadership practices. To remind himself of the importance of overt recognition, he developed a priority list of ways to recognize others. When his team achieved a key milestone, he would go around and personally shake the hand of each and every member of the project team. He would take several key team members out to lunch and make phone calls to all members to thank them personally for their efforts in the project. He'd invite people to a small office party where cake and coffee were served.

Soon after putting a more encouraging leadership approach into place, Moran saw productivity increase, absenteeism decrease, and a stronger human bond developing between coworkers. Furthermore, his own job became easier, as individuals working with him began taking greater initiative. The more cooperative environment led to better communications, with fewer conflicts between staff members. Though there was a great deal of hoopla around the celebrations and recognitions Moran put together, he felt that he should have done even more.

We can all do a lot more. We *must* do a lot more. As the authors of the Kepner-Tregoe study put it, "Unless this issue is addressed, the goal of achieving a high-performance workplace will remain unattainable."[6]

There's more to the explanation of why we don't give and receive more encouragement than the basic assumption that it's part of the job. That's too easy an answer; it doesn't get at the root problem.

Expressing genuine appreciation for the efforts and successes of others means we have to show our emotions. We have to talk about our feelings in public. We have to make ourselves vulnerable to others. For many of us—perhaps most of us—this can be tough, even terrifying.

Take the case of Joan Nicolo, a general manager at a financial services company. For her, encouraging the heart was particularly challenging. She was uncomfortable praising people in public. Yet she knew her direct reports deserved and needed to be acknowledged for the work they were doing. Being a conscientious person, and recognizing that acknowledging others was an important leadership skill, she started asking herself what was holding her back. On the surface, it seemed such a simple task. So what was the big deal?

After considerable soul-searching, she came up with some theories about what she saw as shortcomings in her leadership abilities. For one, she was afraid that if she praised one person, others would think she was playing favorites. She also felt that praising and encouraging activities took too much time. It was just another item to add to her already burgeoning list of responsibilities. But the more she thought about it, the more she realized that her associates really did deserve to be recognized; it was high time to come to terms with her own resistance. She was determined to break through the resistance and give it a try.

A few days later, during a presentation, she made a special point of thanking people publicly for fostering the collaborative spirit of the project they were working on. It felt great, both to her and to others. She said, "I found that my spirit was lifted. They felt appreciated, and I felt that they had received the credit they deserved."

Nicolo felt vulnerable opening herself up like that to thank the group. But she knew for sure that she'd established a human connection with her colleagues that hadn't been there before and would prove to be highly beneficial in the months ahead. Communication was more open after that, and she felt far less guarded than ever before. This was a real turning point for her.

In the following weeks, she brought much more of herself to her work relationships, and people responded with a new level of enthusiasm for her leadership. Indeed, she began to see her coworkers in a different light. She could focus on getting the job done as well as enjoy a human bond with everyone around her. She felt more energetic than ever as she came to work, and when she went home she felt increasing satisfaction with what she'd accomplished. At first it wasn't clear how these changes were going to affect productivity. Would they translate into anything that benefited the company? In a short time, she saw that this new way of relating brought her group together as never before, fueling an esprit de corps that spurred them on to give their personal best whenever an extraordinary effort was required.

Contrary to her worst fears, nobody got jealous when she praised one person or another, and the time it took to show her appreciation was well worth it. Summing up the experience, she said, "I learned that openly celebrating successes is essential to building and sustaining a unified team. Never again will I underrate the importance of encouraging the heart, of visibly appreciating others and their efforts in my future leadership experiences."

We've been misleading ourselves for years, operating according to myths about leadership and management that have kept us from seeing the truth.

First, there's the myth of rugged individualism. There's this belief that individualistic achievement gets us the best results. "If you want something done right," we hear, "do it yourself." We seem content to believe that we really don't need other people to perform at our best.

The fact is, we don't do our best in isolation. We don't get extraordinary things done by working alone with no support, encouragement, expressions of confidence, or help from others. That's not how we make the best decisions, get the best grades, run faster, achieve the highest levels of sales, invent breakthrough products, or live longer.

We've also operated under the myth that leaders ought to be cool, aloof, and analytical; they ought to separate emotion from work. We're told that real leaders don't need love, affection, and friendship. "It's not a popularity contest" is a phrase we've all heard often. "I don't care if people like me. I just want them to respect me."

Nonsense.

One of the most uplifting interviews we conducted in the course of writing this book was with Tony Codianni, director of the Training and Dealer Development Group for Toshiba America Information Systems. Codianni told us that "encouraging the heart is *the* most important leadership practice, because it's the most personal." Codianni believes leadership is all about people, and if you're going to lead people you have to care about them.

Codianni is right.

The Center for Creative Leadership (CCL) in Colorado Springs has taken a look at the process of executive selection, and their results support Codianni's observation. Jodi Taylor, vice president of CCL, told us that in examining the critical variables for success for the top three jobs in large organizations, they found that the number one success factor is "relationships with subordinates."[7]

In an even more startling study, CCL found something that should forever put to rest the myth of the purely rational manager. Using a battery of measurement instruments,[8] CCL researchers looked at a number of factors that could account for a manager's success. CCL found that one, and *only* one, factor significantly differentiated the top quartile of managers from the bottom quartile. (They found it on an assessment instrument called FIRO-B, developed by William C. Schutz. The FIRO-B measures two aspects of three basic interpersonal needs: the extent to which we express and we want inclusion, control, and affection.[9])

What was the factor that distinguished highest-performing managers from lowest-performing? The popular assumption about managers is that they have a high need to express control. So you might think that's the factor that distinguishes highest- from lowest-performing managers. But that's *not* what CCL found. Rather, the single factor that differentiated the top from the bottom was higher scores on *affection*—both expressed and wanted. Contrary to the myth of the cold-hearted boss who cares very little about people's feelings, the highest-performing managers show more warmth and fondness toward others than do the bottom 25 percent. They get closer to people, and they're significantly more open in sharing thoughts and feelings than their lower-performing counterparts.

Now, these managers were not without their rational sides. In fact, on another measure administered by CCL they all scored high on "thinking," and on their need to have power and influence over others. It's just that these factors didn't explain why managers were higher performers.

When the CCL researchers examined their findings more closely, they found that the highest-performing managers' subordinates *two levels down* in the organization were significantly more satisfied overall with their coworkers, supervision, top leaders, organization planning, ethics, and quality. Clearly, openness and affection pay off.

The CCL study adds to the growing body of evidence that *emotional intelligence* can be more important than IQ in predicting success in organizations—or in life, for that matter. Daniel Goleman, in his groundbreaking book on the subject, refers to *emotional intelligence* (EQ) as "a master aptitude, a capacity that profoundly affects all other abilities, either facilitating or interfering with them."[10] Elsewhere, Goleman says that of the five dimensions of EQ, empathy is "the fundamental skill of management."[11]

Even more intriguing in the CCL study is the finding that the highest-performing managers also had higher-than-average scores on *wanted affection*. In fact, the average *wanted affection* score on the FIRO-B is the highest of all the scores!

Yet, as CCL's Jodi Taylor related it to us, in all the years she's been collecting data on leaders—there are more than thirty thousand leaders in its database—she's "never had a group that expressed more affection than it wanted." It seems we all want more affection than we give. Reflecting on this finding, she comments that "everybody is waiting for someone else to show them affection." The question is, what are we waiting for? What are *you* waiting for?

We've all heard the dismissing comment made by many in the managerial ranks that "I don't care what people think of me." Well, it may indeed be true for them, but it's not true of the best leaders. The best leaders want to be liked, and they want openness from other people. Not caring how others feel and think about what we do and say is an attitude for losers— an attitude that can only lead to less and less effectiveness.

The evidence tells us that expressing affection is important to success, *and* we have high needs for it; it's as if we're all trying to hide something that we all want. We have a secret we're afraid to reveal because it might make us look soft or wimpy or who knows what. *The secret is this: we all really do want to be loved.*

Some years back, when we interviewed former chief executive officer and now venture capitalist Irwin Federman, his remarks foreshadowed what we now know from the data. He spoke an important truth about the *chemistry* that exists between great leaders and those who follow them. He spoke of love as a necessary ingredient, one that is rarely appreciated, in part because we underrate the role of our feelings.

Reflecting on our love for our leaders, Federman said: "You don't love someone because of who they are; you love them because of the way they make you feel. This axiom applies equally in a company setting. It may seem inappropriate to use words such as *love* and *affection* in relation to business. Conventional wisdom has it that management is not a popularity contest. . . . I contend, however, that all things being equal, we will work harder and more effectively for people we like. And we like them in direct proportion to how they make us feel."[12]

It is impossible to escape the message here that if people work with leaders who encourage the heart, they feel better about themselves. Their self-esteem goes up. These leaders set people's spirits free, often inspiring them to become more than they ever thought possible. This, indeed, may be our ultimate mission as leaders.

In his book *The Heart Aroused,* David Whyte talks a great deal about the "vital side of our self that is repressed and sometimes strangled" by the corporate world.[13] He says that in banishing this vital part of ourselves in the name of "safety and good sense," we find that "our capacity for vitality and enthusiasm is lost." It's this vitality and enthusiasm that leaders can awaken in people. But to awaken it in others, they must first awaken their own enthusiasm in the workplace and express it openly.

To awaken vitality in others, Whyte points out, leaders have to cross a certain boundary between themselves and their associates. Sometimes it's not easy, because most of us have been raised to believe that it's important to maintain a buffer of "safety and good sense" between ourselves and the people who choose to follow our leadership. Perhaps the greatest risk we take as leaders is losing the interpersonal safety zone. If we don't open up to others and express our affection and appreciation, then we stay safe behind the wall of rationality. But as the CCL folks have learned, it's not an either-or. We have minds *and* hearts. Both are meant to be used at work. When we use them both, we're more effective. To use our minds and not our hearts is to deny ourselves greater success.

JUST SAY THANK-YOU

Opening up is harder for some people than for others, but major psychotherapy is not required here. It starts with what Robert Fulghum pointed out some years ago in his book *Everything I Ever Needed to Know I Learned in Kindergarten*[14]: the little reminder pinned to the wall where you're sure to see it every morning when you come to work: "Remember to say thank you!"

Study after study points out just how fundamental all this really is. For example, one survey examining employee turnover found that the chief reason people give for leaving is that they get "limited praise and recognition."[15] When asked what skills their managers might develop to be more effective, employees place at the top of the list "the ability to recognize and acknowledge the contributions of others."

This is not new news. In 1949, a famous study by Lawrence Lindahl asked employees to rank the intangible rewards of their jobs. Then their managers were asked to rank what they believed the employees wanted.[16]

Highest on the employees' lists were (1) feeling appreciated, and (2) feeling that they were being informed about things that were happening. They wanted to be listened to. And what did their managers think this same group of employees wanted? They believed their employees would put good wages, job security, and advancement opportunities first. In fact, most managers had no idea how highly their employees valued being appreciated and feeling that they were informed and listened to.

You might say, "Well, that was 1949; a lot has changed since then." We would certainly agree with you; a lot has changed. But a lot has not. Lindahl repeated his study of employees and managers in the 1980s, and again in the 1990s. The results? Each time, the findings came out the same.

What about the managers themselves? How did they rank these intangible rewards of the workplace? Like the employees they supervised, managers ranked being appreciated, informed, and listened to highest on their lists. But why should this surprise us? Managers, leaders, employees: everyone is human. We all have these needs to feel that we matter, to feel that those with whom we work appreciate what we have to give and that they value us enough to let us know what's going on.

In preparing this book, we did our own survey and asked people to identify the most important nonfinancial reward they receive at work. The most common answer was a simple thank-you. Author Gerald H. Graham reports that personal congratulations rank at the top of the most powerful nonfinancial motivators identified by employees.[17] Harvard Business School professor Rosabeth Moss Kanter reports that in the most innovative companies there is a significantly higher volume of thank-yous than in companies of low innovation.[18]

Appreciation, acknowledgment, praise, thank-yous, some simple gesture that says, "I care about you and what you do." That's how we start. Whether in the form of a simple thank-you or an elaborate celebration, encouragement is feedback— positive feedback. It's information that communicates "You're on the right track. You're doing really well. Thanks." To deny each other this gift of positive feedback is to deny increased opportunities for success.

Of course, there's more to it than this. In the next chapter, we take a look at a classic case of one leader as a way of teaching us the rudiments of encouraging the heart. We also learn the fundamental principles that are essential to offering genuine encouragement to others.

As you read further, though, keep in mind the basic message of this chapter: at the heart of effective leadership is genuinely caring for people.

CHAPTER TWO

The Seven Essentials
of Encouraging

All the goodness, beauty, and perfection of a human being belong
to the one who knows how to recognize these qualities.
— GEORGETTE LEBLANC, English actress and poet

W hile he was president of North American Tool and Die
(NATD), Tom Melohn enjoyed giving out Super Person of the Month awards to employees who went the
extra mile to help the company move toward its goal of high
quality and no product rejects. Melohn made himself highly
visible to everyone in the workplace. But more than this, he
personally presented the Super Person awards with a gregari-
ous style that was his trademark. Because of his high level of
engagement with the people around him, people felt they knew
him. He put himself out there fearlessly, giving his leadership
a little extra pizzazz, which tended to be mirrored back to him
in the enthusiasm people brought to the workplace. Through
the strength of his presence, Melohn revealed that he knew
what was going on, and that he cared about people, got a great
deal of pleasure from his work, and took pride in the accomplishments of others.

Over the years, we've used Melohn as our best-practices
example of how a leader can encourage the heart. One specific

incident in particular, in just two minutes, truly exemplifies all the essential principles and actions that form the foundation of this practice. In this description of a Super Person award ceremony, pay particular attention to how Melohn interacts with Kelly and "the gang," as Melohn affectionately calls them, who have gathered to witness the award presentation. Notice the level of delight Melohn expresses, and how he engages everyone in the room through his questions and by adding dramatic elements to the celebration. As you read this case example, see what *essentials* you can tease from it. We'll be discussing them throughout the book.

This scene takes place on the shop floor of NATD. Employees are gathered in the employee break area near the boxes and machinery of the plant, for a Super Person of the Month award.[1]

"We've got a new award today," Melohn announces to the assembled group. "It's called the North American Tool and Die 'Freezer' Award. Now, who knows what that's for and who won it? Anybody? Anybody got an idea?"

Somebody shouts out: "Kelly!"

"There's something in the freezer," Melohn says. "Kelly . . . go on, Kelly, look in the freezer. Go on. Come on. Hurry up!"

Kelly opens the door of a freezer standing nearby and reaches inside. He finds a metal rod and cylinder. There's an envelope stuck to them.

Melohn laughs. "Come on up here."

Everyone joins in the joy and laughter as Kelly walks up and Melohn shakes his hand. Melohn laughs some more, obviously delighted with the fun the group is having at this ceremony. Melohn takes the envelope and metal rod out of Kelly's hand.

"Oh, that's cold!" Melohn exclaims. He hands the envelope back to Kelly and sets the metal part on a table.

Kelly opens the envelope and pulls out a check for fifty dollars.

"Okay?" Melohn asks Kelly.

"Yeah!" Kelly says, smiling shyly.

"Remember this job?" Melohn asks the group. "I went through the shop one day and I saw Kelly going in the freezer. I thought, 'What the hell is going on? Is he goofing off or making margaritas for Joe, or what?' You know what he did? He couldn't get this (Melohn points to the metal rod) into here (he points to the metal cylinder), so he said, 'Hey, I'm going to put this in the freezer. It'll shrink, and then I'll put the part together.' And it worked! And I said, 'Where in the hell did you get that idea?' He said, 'What? It's just part of the job, right?'" Melohn looks at Kelly.

"Yep," Kelly says.

Melohn turns to Kelly, puts his arm around his shoulder, and says, "What else can I say, gang? God love you, baby. God love you." Then he turns to the group, holds the part in the air, and says, with pride and caring in his voice: "And remember: no rejects, no rejects, no rejects! That's why we're here, gang."

If you'd like to watch this scene and an in-depth interview with Melohn about leadership and employee partnership, they're in the film *In Search of Excellence: The Video.*[2]

We've asked thousands of people in our classes and workshops to watch the Melohn case on video and tell us what they observe. We tell them that if they can learn to incorporate what Melohn did into their daily leadership actions, they'll earn nearly perfect scores on encouraging the heart.

What precisely did Tom Melohn do? What actions did he take? What words did he use? What nonverbal behaviors did he exhibit? What values did he exemplify that encouraged the heart? Here are some of the viewers' representative responses:

He was genuine; he was a real person.

He saw Kelly do this; he was out on the shop floor, and he took note of it.

He showed that he believed in people.

He put his arm around Kelly.

He really loved his employees.

He made it fun.

He recognized Kelly in public, not behind a closed door in his office.

He told a story about Kelly.

He didn't just talk about recognition, he lived it.

He gave out the award himself; he didn't delegate it.

He was clear about the standards: total quality.

He repeated the statement "no rejects" several times.

He gave Kelly a check, sharing some of the organization's benefit from Kelly's action.

He was laughing and having a good time. He really enjoyed recognizing Kelly.

As these observations testify, close analysis of the NATD "Freezer" Award ceremony (and others like it) teaches us that underlying the practice of encouraging the heart there is a set of recognizable, learnable, and repeatable actions leaders take that both make people feel special and reinforce the standards of the enterprise. From people's observations, we've identified seven essentials to encouraging the heart. When leaders do their best to encourage the heart, they:

1. Set clear standards
2. Expect the best
3. Pay attention
4. Personalize recognition
5. Tell the story
6. Celebrate together
7. Set the example

Let's take a closer look at the Melohn case so that we can fully illuminate the essentials of encouraging the heart.

SET CLEAR STANDARDS

At the close of the Super Person of the Month ceremony, Tom Melohn said something that is crucial to understanding how to be most effective in encouraging the heart: "Remember: no rejects, no rejects, no rejects! That's why we're here, gang."

Melohn had a clear set of standards that he expected people in the organization to live up to. Whether he was walking the floor, making a presentation, talking to a customer, or holding a meeting, he and others knew what the expectations were. The most important for NATD was *no rejects!* None, zero, nada, not one. It was why they were in business. Anything less in the highly competitive market they served meant loss, and maybe the death, of business.

In recognizing individuals, we sometimes get lost in the ceremonial aspects. We think about form, but we forget substance. Recognitions are reminders; quite literally, the word *recognize* comes from the Latin to "know again." Recognitions are opportunities to say to everyone, "I'd like to remind you one more time what's important around here. Here's what we value. Now, let me give you one example of how someone in this organization demonstrated what it means to meet or exceed our standards."

The first prerequisite, then, to encouraging the heart is to set clear standards. The standards were as much the focus of the freezer award as was the action that won Kelly his reward. In this entertaining moment, Melohn linked the reward with the standards that had been set. The reward was for an action in service of a clear purpose.

To be successful in encouraging the heart, it's absolutely

critical that everyone cherish a common set of standards. (We've chosen to use the word *standards* to mean goals as well as values or principles.) It's certainly not very encouraging to be in the dark about what we're expected to achieve, or never to know where we stand relative to what's important. Only when we know the standards can we set our sights for success. By clearly defining the values and principles for which we're held accountable and by linking performance to those standards, leaders establish a benchmark for achievement.

However, not just any standards will do. They must be standards of excellence. They must be aspirational, and bring out the best in us. They must make us feel like winners when we attain them. Certainly, "no rejects" is a lot more aspirational and inspirational than, say, "Five out of ten will do."

Melohn may have ended his presentation to Kelly with the statement about no rejects, but he also began with it—in his mind. Everyone knew what was expected. Repeating the standard at the end was just one more way of reinforcing the values that everyone, ahead of time, knew were important. Repetition is a powerful pedagogical device. By repeating the standard, Melohn reinforces a crucial principle for employees of North American Tool and Die. He links appropriate performance to the reward, signaling that if one follows this model of behavior then other rewards follow.

EXPECT THE BEST

Every time we watch this video segment, several people invariably comment on how genuine Melohn is, how much he cares, how much he really believes that the people on the front line can achieve a standard of no rejects. Describing the practices of leadership, Melohn puts it this way: "In my judgment, the best leaders have two characteristics. The first is an unswerving, single-minded, utterly all-consuming set of values not unlike the NATD currencies. The second, shared trait of leaders is a similar perception of people. Over and over again, they express their belief in the innate goodness of human beings. All the energies of the best leaders—in fact, their entire lives—are dedicated to helping people achieve their full potential."[3]

Melohn is right. The best leaders believe that no matter what their role, people can achieve the high standards that have been set. It's called the Pygmalion effect, a belief so strong that even if others don't believe in themselves initially, the leader's belief—or the teacher's or parent's or colleague's—gives rise to self-confidence, to a belief that "Yes, I *can* do it." It becomes a "self-fulfilling prophecy."

Belief in others' abilities is fundamental to encouraging the heart. Like it or not, our beliefs about people are broadcast in ways we're not even aware of. We just give off certain cues that say to people either "You can do it, I know you can do it" or "There's no way you'll ever be able to do that." How can you expect someone to get extraordinary things done if she picks up the signal that you don't believe she can? Even if you said, "Thanks, great job," how genuine would it be perceived to be?

As we describe later, when leaders expect people to achieve, they do. When they label people underachievers, performance suffers. Passionately believing in people and expecting the best of them is another prerequisite to encouraging the heart.

PAY ATTENTION

"I went through the shop one day. . . ." Melohn told us. This gives us an immediate clue as to the kind of leader he is. He's a wanderer, a walk-arounder, a leader who is right there with you. He's a leader in the truest sense of the word—a venturer. We quickly learn from the little scene at NATD that Melohn is a leader who delights in "catching people doing things right."

But it's more than that just *catching* people doing things right, it's also *paying attention* and understanding the significance of their actions. All too often, we notice something happening but we ignore it. We just pass on by or file it away, thinking to ourselves that we'll get to it later. Melohn's own description of this practice tells us the difference. You've probably heard of MBWA, managing by walking around. Melohn calls it CBWA: *caring* by walking around. A one-word difference, but what a word. Caring just feels different than managing, now, doesn't it?

As Melohn tells the story, on one of his CBWA tours he noticed Kelly doing something unusual. At that point, he could have ignored what was going on. But being curious and because he cared, he didn't. Instead, he went up to Kelly, started asking questions, and engaged him in conversation. Learning what Kelly was doing, Melohn understood that this man's actions were the very embodiment of the standards NATD wanted people to maintain. He was so impressed by Kelly's going the extra mile that he decided to make a positive example of him. By telling Kelly's story, he would encourage the heart of everyone there to hook up their work efforts to the value of no rejects.

We must add something. Even though he was owner and, as he referred to himself, "head sweeper," of NATD, Melohn wasn't the one to pick the Super Person winners. Supervisors and foremen nominated candidates once a week, and that same group chose the monthly winner. Melohn would occasionally make suggestions, but his wasn't the deciding vote. This is even more reason why paying attention is so important. Melohn could have passed the incident by because he wasn't the one who would pick the award winners. But he cared enough to notice, invest the attention, and persuade others of the merits.

Leaders are always on the lookout for exemplars of the values and standards. Wherever they are, whatever they're doing, the best leaders have a special radar that picks up positive signals.

PERSONALIZE RECOGNITION

Notice what Melohn did to make this award special for Kelly. While the Super Person of the Month was a regular feature at NATD when Melohn was there, this award was special. He gave it a unique, attention-getting name: the North American Tool and Die "Freezer" Award, tying it specifically to something that Kelly—and nobody else—had done. Melohn *personalized* it. He customized the award and the ceremony just for Kelly.

Melohn didn't stand up in front of the room and say, "Today I want to present Kelly with an award for working to achieve the company standard of no rejects. Here's a check, Kelly. Thanks." Instead, he choreographed the whole thing. He put the metal part in the freezer so that when the time came Kelly would go back to the freezer, open it, and take out the part. This is clearly not something that happens every day. The fact that it was unusual, fun, and dramatic all helps to imprint the event and the stated values in people's minds.

This emphasis on the individual uplifts Kelly and sends the message to others that singular efforts really can make a difference. We've learned time and time again that people have become cynical about perfunctory thank-yous and gold watches. We've collected cases where people even received something of great monetary value, but because the leader hadn't put any thought into it, hadn't considered the *individual* who was being recognized, the effect was the opposite of what was intended. It didn't inspire the person to do his best; rather it convinced him that the leader really didn't know him and didn't really care about him. The leader was doing it because she learned somewhere that what leaders were supposed to do was encourage others.

Before recognizing someone, then, the best leaders get to know people personally. They learn about their likes and dislikes, their needs and interests. They observe them in their own settings. Then, when it comes time to recognize a particular person, they know a way to make it special, meaningful, and memorable.

TELL THE STORY

Storytelling is one of the oldest ways in the world to convey the values and ideals shared by a community. Before the written word, stories were the means for passing along the important lessons of life. We know how important they are in teaching children, but sometimes we forget how important they are to adults. In fact, research tells us that stories have more of an impact on whether businesspeople believe information than do straight data.[4] Venture capitalists (some of the most numbers-driven people on the planet) always talk about how important "the story" is when taking a company public and selling the initial public offering to Wall Street.

The story is just as crucial to encouraging the heart. But why tell the story? Why not just bring Kelly up, give him the check and public recognition, and then have him sit down? Why take the time to reenact what was done? What difference does it make?

Well, let's see. Here's how the ceremony might have gone without the story.

> "We've got another Super Person award today," Melohn announces. "Let's see, who won it? Uh, Kelly. Kelly won it. Come on up here, Kelly."
>
> Everyone watches passively as Kelly walks up to the front of the room. Melohn hands Kelly the monthly Super Person plaque and a check for fifty dollars.
>
> "Thank you Kelly," Melohn says matter-of-factly. "You really showed us what it means to implement our policy of zero defects."
>
> "Remember," he continues, turning emotionlessly to the group, "no rejects, no rejects, no rejects! That's why we're here, gang."

Yawn. Not only is this boring, but everyone, including Kelly, will forget about it the instant it's over. There's absolutely nothing in this rendering that's memorable.

The intention of stories is not just to entertain. Oh, they're intended to do that for sure. But they're also intended to teach. The influential educator and philosopher Marshall McLuhan is reported to have said, "Those who think there's a difference between education and entertainment don't know the first thing about either one."

Good stories move us. They touch us, they teach us, and they cause us to remember. They enable the listener to put the behavior in a real context and understand what has to be done in that context to live up to expectations. By telling the story in detail, Melohn was illustrating what *everyone*, not just Kelly, could do to live by the standard of no rejects. In effect, he was saying, "Whenever you encounter a situation like this, do as Kelly did. Knowing that we value zero rejects around here,

Kelly didn't want to waste even one part. So he thought about what he could do to live up to that standard. You can do the same in your job." Melohn wanted people who faced similar opportunities to say to themselves, "Well, when Kelly was faced with that problem, he took personal initiative to find a solution. Now, let me see what I can do."

Melohn could have said all that didactically, but he didn't. He just told the story. Not only did he tell the story, he actually got Kelly to reenact a portion of it, much like a skilled director on the set of a movie. The story captures our attention and excites and entertains us. Even while capturing our attention, the narration of what happened provides a behavioral map that people can easily store in their minds. We get the message, and we remember it far longer than if he gave us a lecture on total quality management.

Besides giving us context, good stories do another thing for us. They enable us to see ourselves. We learn best from those we can most relate to—people most like ourselves. CEO stories might be good examples for other CEOs, or to those who aspire to that job, but they're not very good examples for people on the shop floor. It's not that CEOs can't be good examples, but people can't relate to someone who's not like them. Besides, there's only one CEO per organization, while there are a lot of folks in other roles. We need to hear stories about those other folks if we're going to learn how to behave.

Although the live example is the most powerful of ways to publicize what people do to exemplify values, there are other media available to leaders. Newsletters, annual reports, advertisements, even voice mail and e-mail can be used to encourage the heart and teach positive stories about what people do to exemplify our values. These media sure are a lot more powerful than posting our values on a wall somewhere.

Melohn could have called Kelly into his office and privately thanked him. However, far more is achieved by recognizing him in public. There's no point in simply telling the story in private; Kelly already knows what he did. The story is more for the benefit of others. It's how groups learn lessons. The public ceremony provides a setting for broadcasting the message to a much wider audience.

Many of us are reluctant to recognize people in public situations like this, perhaps fearing that it might cause jealousy or resentment. That's one of the things that initially prevented Joan Nicolo from doing more encouraging (as we saw in the preceding chapter). But if the leader is genuine, this doesn't happen. Teresa Bettencourt, a production worker at NATD, once remarked about the Super Person award: "You feel great. You really go home and say, 'Hey, I must be pretty good. I got to be Super Person this time.' You would think that there would be some people who would say, 'How come she got it and I didn't?' But no. Everybody is happy when somebody gets it."[5]

Most of us want others to know about our achievements, and the public ceremony does that, sparing us the need to go around bragging about ourselves. The experience of leaders who recognize others publicly is that it rarely causes hard feelings, and in most cases it helps bring people closer.

Imagine for a moment that Melohn does call Kelly into his office and gives the award privately. If Melohn believes that doing so publicly will create jealousy among the workers, the scene might go something like this:

> "Kelly, I heard that you did something to help our efforts to achieve our goal of no rejects. To thank you for your initiative, here's a check for fifty dollars."

"Thanks," says Kelly. They shake hands, and as Kelly walks out the door, Melohn stops him and says, "One more thing. Please don't tell anyone else you got this. It might cause some friction on the floor, and we don't want that."

Kelly may have fifty extra bucks in his pocket, but he's also got a burden. He can't tell anyone. He can't be proud of himself and what he's done. He can't receive the high-fives and the "Way to go, Kelly!" congratulations because he can't say anything. The opportunity has also been lost to teach a valuable lesson by example. This is no way to create an atmosphere of encouragement. Just the opposite.

We see in Melohn and Kelly's story that ceremonies of this kind are hardly frills or luxuries that we can dispense with in the work-a-day world. Today's leaders are discovering that encouraging the heart through public events builds trust and strengthens relationships in the workplace. By lifting the spirits of people in this way, we heighten awareness of organization expectations and humanize the values and standards such that we motivate at a deep and enduring level. But even more, public recognition serves as a valuable educational mechanism demonstrating company values and encouraging others to duplicate the actions that they see rewarded.

Public ceremonies serve another powerful purpose. They bring people closer together. As we move to a more virtual world, where communication is by voice mail, e-mail, cell phone, videoconference, and pager, it's becoming ever more difficult for people to find opportunities to be together. We are social animals, and we need each other. Those who are fortunate enough to have lots of social support are healthier human beings than those who have little. Social support is absolutely essential to our well-being and to our productivity. Celebrating together is one way we can get this essential support.

You can't delegate encouraging the heart. Every leader in the organization—every person, in fact—has to take the initiative to recognize individual contributions, celebrate team accomplishments, and create an atmosphere of confidence and support. It's not something we should wait around for others to do. "Do unto others as you would have them do unto you" clearly applies here. The foundation of leadership, as we have already said, is credibility. What is credibility behaviorally? Over and over again, people tell us credibility is "doing what you say you will do." Leaders *set the example* for others. They practice what they preach. If you want others to encourage the heart, you start by modeling it yourself.

That's certainly what Melohn did. *He* set high standards. *He* believed in others. *He* invested his attention in others through CBWA. *He* personalized the recognition. *He* told the stories. *He* celebrated with others. *He* set the example. You can't expect others in the organization to follow your lead if you don't take the first step yourself.

Personal involvement is also a genuine expression of caring. It helps foster trust and partnership. Leadership cannot be exercised from a distance. Leadership is a relationship, and relationships are formed only when people come into contact with each other.

Melohn also put his money where his mouth is in other ways. He made the recognition tangible by presenting Kelly with a check for fifty dollars and putting Kelly's name on a plaque that went on public display. By themselves, the check and plaque didn't significantly contribute to sustaining the value of the action in people's minds. However, when combined with all the rest, these tangible rewards helped memorialize the event. The money, though certainly not a fortune, confirmed that the organization took the action seriously and was willing to share some of its gain with Kelly. The plaque offered a constant reminder to everyone that the organization values people who demonstrate the behaviors consistent with the values and standards.

P.S.: let's not confuse Melohn's positive role modeling as an example of someone who's "soft." Zero defects is a very tough standard. CBWA is a demanding practice. Effective communication, if you're serious about it, requires dedication and self-control. Public displays of emotion are not for the fainthearted. It's become well known that people are more frightened of public speaking than they are of dying. Supporting others, particularly in times of great change, can be physically and emotionally draining.

It may seem easy, but we have learned that encouraging the heart is one of the two most difficult of the five practices of exemplary leadership. We've found that it's much easier for leaders to challenge the process, for example, than it is for them to encourage the heart. There's still a lot leaders have to learn.

We begin to see from all this that the seven essentials of encouraging the heart are core leadership skills. They are not just about showing people they can win for the sake of making them feel good. This is a curiously serious business. When striving to raise quality, recover from disaster, start up a new service, or make dramatic change of any kind, leaders must make sure that people experience in their hearts that what they do matters.

MOVING FORWARD

There's no better way to begin learning than to assess where you are now against some standard. It gives you a baseline for improvement. To give you that opportunity, we've elaborated on the encouraging-the-heart factor from our *Leadership Practices Inventory* and created a twenty-one item Encouragement Index (in the next chapter). By going quickly through this brief assessment tool, you develop a picture of your strengths and opportunities for improvement in the area of encouraging the heart. This inventory is intended to help you identify where to put your energy so as to produce the greatest improvements in the shortest period of time.

CHAPTER THREE

The Encouragement Index

Pity the leader who is caught between unloving critics and uncritical lovers.

—JOHN GARDNER, *On Leadership*

hen we began researching leadership, we chose to focus on how ordinary people, not celebrities with high visibility, were able to lead others to accomplish extraordinary things. We saw that most of us perform special feats in our own lives and regularly inspire others. We wanted to know what people just like you do to lead others to places they've never been before.

We saw, over and over again, that leadership doesn't depend on mystical qualities or inborn gifts but rather on the capacity of individuals to know themselves, their strengths, and their weaknesses, and to learn from the feedback they get in their daily lives—in short, their capacity for self-improvement.

Leadership scholars consistently note the high correlation between leadership skills and the capacity for self-improvement. Warren Bennis observes that "'know thyself' is the inscription over the oracle at Delphi. And it's still the most difficult task any of us faces. But until you truly know yourself, your strengths and weaknesses, know what you want to do and why you want to do it, you cannot succeed in any but the most superficial sense of the word."[1]

Nearly twenty years have passed since we began our work, and during that time we've gathered volumes of information. We have more than twenty-five hundred cases and one hundred thousand survey responses in our database. From all these data, we've concluded that leadership can be learned. Leadership development is self-development: getting feedback in our daily lives, setting self-improvement goals, learning from others and from experience, making changes in how we do things so as to continuously expand our ability, and then getting more feedback to check our progress.

To know what to change in our lives, we need to understand what we're doing that is getting the results we want and what we're doing that is not. It's important to hold a positive perspective in mind; if you are in a leadership position now, or striving for such a role, the chances are excellent that you're doing so because you or someone else in your life has recognized your leadership potential. To fully liberate that potential and put it into action, you need a pretty good picture of your strengths and how to build upon them.

To help you along the path of self-development, we've taken our *Leadership Practices Inventory* (LPI),[2] which measures all five practices of exemplary leadership, and expanded on the items that measure encouraging the heart. Our Encouragement Index (EI) is in the next section; we urge you to take a few minutes to assess yourself before reading more about each of the essentials. The EI is strictly a self-evaluation process, so take your time with it.

THE ENCOURAGEMENT INDEX

The Encouragement Index (Exhibit 3.1) lists twenty-one statements about what leaders do to encourage the heart. Read each statement carefully, and then, using the 10-point scale, indicate how often you typically engage in each behavior. Evaluate yourself on the basis of your present behavior, that is, what you're doing right now, not from the vantage point of what you think you should be doing or where you'd like to be in the near future.

Rate yourself numerically on each behavior by writing the appropriate number in the blank space to the left of each statement. For example, if you think you engage in the behavior "once in a while," then write a 4 in the blank. If you think you engage in the behavior "often," then write a 7 in the blank.

Note: you don't have to be in a management position to engage in these behaviors. Remember, leadership is everyone's business.

SCORING THE ENCOURAGEMENT INDEX

There's a rule in golf that applies equally to self-improvement: *play it as it lies.* For you nongolfers, that simply means that you have to play the ball from wherever it lands, whether it's in the rough or on the green ten inches from the cup. Applied to self-improvement, the notion suggests that we have to be able to identify and look very honestly at *where we are right now* in terms of our skills. The information we gather in this way tells us where to start correcting, where to start building our skills, and how to make the most of our strengths. As every good navigator knows, you've got to know where you're starting out or the chances are good that you'll never reach your destination.

Exhibit 3.1. The Encouragement Index.

How frequently do you typically engage in this behavior? Write the number from the scale below that best describes your response to each statement.

1	2	3	4	5
Almost never	Rarely	Seldom	Once in a while	Sometimes

1. _____ I make certain we set a standard that motivates us to do better in the future than we are doing now.
2. _____ I express high expectations about what people are capable of accomplishing.
3. _____ I pay more attention to the positive things people do than to the negative.
4. _____ I personally acknowledge people for their contributions.
5. _____ I tell stories about the special achievements of the members of the team.
6. _____ I make sure that our group celebrates accomplishments together.
7. _____ I get personally involved when we recognize the achievements of others.
8. _____ I clearly communicate my personal values and professional standards to everyone on the team.
9. _____ I let people know I have confidence in their abilities.
10. _____ I spend a good deal of time listening to the needs and interests of other people.
11. _____ I personalize the recognition I give to another person.
12. _____ I find opportunities to let people know the *why* behind whatever we are doing.
13. _____ I hold special events to celebrate our successes.

6	7	8	9	10
Fairly often	Often	Usually	Very often	Almost always

14. ____ I show others, by my own example, how people should be recognized and rewarded.
15. ____ I make it a point to give people feedback on how they are performing against our agreed-upon standards.
16. ____ I express a positive and optimistic outlook even when times are tough.
17. ____ I get to know, at a personal level, the people with whom I work.
18. ____ I find creative ways to make my recognition of others unique and special.
19. ____ I recognize people more in public than in private for their exemplary performance.
20. ____ I find ways to make the workplace enjoyable and fun.
21. ____ I personally congratulate people for a job well done.

____ TOTAL (add together all the ratings above; the lowest possible total you can have is 21, and the highest is 210)

The Encouragement Index

Once you've done the scoring at the bottom of the EI, rank yourself according to the following explanations of your score.

From 186 to 210

You're doing great! You're probably seeing a lot of your associates producing at high levels. Morale is high. People like working with you because you keep the work environment upbeat and positive, maybe even inspiring. They feel appreciated and are feeling good about the contribution they are making.

Encouraging the heart appears to be a highly developed part of your leadership repertoire. Your presence alone is an asset. If you're not already doing it, look around for someone who could use your mentoring abilities to be as effective as you are at encouraging others. Also, if people aren't already taking the initiative to recognize and celebrate on their own, use your skills to provide structures and tools so they don't have to wait for you to get the ball rolling. Let them know it would be great if they, too, would encourage and celebrate others' achievements.

Finally, always be on the lookout for new ways to encourage the heart, to avoid becoming too repetitive, predictable, or boring.

From 126 to 185

You're doing pretty darn well. Although most of your associates are producing, you may have the feeling that they could be giving more. You know there might be some grumbling, but people are generally happy working with you. You may have the haunting feeling from time to time that there is something more you could be doing to motivate and encourage people, but you don't know exactly what it is.

You clearly recognize that encouraging the heart is important, yet you may feel reluctant to commit completely to this practice daily. To take the next step, ask yourself what's holding you back from encouraging more. For example, some people put limits on how much they encourage others because they feel that leaders need to keep a certain emotional distance from the others. You discover as you proceed, though, that you can keep a certain distance even as you are acknowledging individuals and celebrating your team's accomplishments.

Perhaps you're just not the cheerleader type, and you're turned off by the idea of making too much of what people are getting paid to do; you feel that they shouldn't be expecting any special treatment. Even if there is some truth in this, the fact remains that we are social animals and most of us respond well when we're acknowledged for our efforts.

Whatever the reason you're holding back, take an honest look at it and weigh the reason against what you can gain by encouraging the heart. You might just find that your uneasiness about this process fades away as you experience greater success and ease with this aspect of leadership.

From 66 to 125

People are probably not working to their highest levels, and there's a part of you that is well aware of this fact. You might even get the feeling that the only time everyone is working to capacity is when they think you're watching them. Not to worry, though; there are plenty of tips in the remaining pages for you to put into practice, and then you're well on your way to becoming adept at encouraging the hearts of others.

You may be feeling that there is value in encouraging the heart, but you're missing opportunities to put the practice into motion. Start paying attention to the achievements of the people around you that you feel are worthy of acknowledgment or celebration: a person going the extra mile to complete a project on time, a team within your organization completing a challenging task, or a person just doing something thoughtful that makes your job easier. Your recognition can run the gamut from a simple thank-you to an elaborate celebration.

If you feel reluctant to do any of this, see if you can identify what's holding you back. Lighten up! Think about things you can do to make your workplace more fun and inspiring to people who work there—and more fun and inspiring for you, too, we might add. Even a laugh or two can enhance productivity and worker satisfaction.

From 21 to 65

Our guess is that your score isn't this low. If it is, we hope you'll get busy putting the ideas in this book into practice immediately. If your score is this low, it's a pretty good bet that there is a fair amount of discontent in the ranks, or you're really tough on yourself. The good news is that you are in a position to make immense changes that not only increase productivity but make your job a heck of a lot easier.

We know from our research that most people produce more in an environment where they get positive feedback, and productivity diminishes where there is little or no feedback or where they only hear from their leaders if something is wrong. Since it's your job as a leader to make sure people are earning their keep, you are probably not earning yours unless you are encouraging the heart.

Make a commitment today to find something in your workplace to celebrate. Say thank you to someone who enables you to be a little more effective—and tell them so! Perhaps you don't appreciate how important encouraging the heart is for maintaining the vitality of your team. Or maybe you're just overlooking opportunities to celebrate and give recognition. See if there is someone else in your organization you can team up with to help encourage others. Find a role model and spend some time with that person as you learn from her how she encourages the heart.

True leadership has its own intrinsic rewards; they come as you learn to work with others not through intimidation and control but through cooperation and recognition.

BOOSTING YOUR SCORE

In the process of rating yourself, of course, not only do you gain some insights into how much or how little you're encouraging the hearts of others but you also automatically get some ideas about ways to improve. For example, if you rated yourself low on question number 1, simply start looking for more opportunities to praise people. Low on number 5? Look for ways to celebrate accomplishments. In most cases, you don't have to leave the workplace to begin boosting your EI rating as far as encouraging the heart is concerned.

As you move on to the next seven chapters in this book, you'll find lessons and positive examples of how actual leaders implement each of the seven essentials of encouraging the heart. In each chapter there are examples, discussions, and suggestions for achieving the leadership goals we describe in this book. It's not our intention that everyone should master all seven essentials before bringing them into the workplace. On the contrary: new habits are built one small step at a time.

The very next step before you should be the one that, after glancing over all seven, you find yourself naturally drawn to.

The Encouragement Index

This might be because you're already taking action in this area, or because you've concluded it's your weakest point and one you need to start working on right now. Trust your intuition to choose the next *right* step.

PART TWO

CHAPTER FOUR

The First Essential
Set Clear Standards

You have to have the discipline, and then you'll be liberated by it.
— PETER HALL, former director, National Theatre of England

W e met Tony Codianni, of Toshiba America, in Chapter One. He once told us: "I have a need to be personal with my folks. To me there's no difference between work and personal life. . . . Encouraging comes from the heart. It's heart-to-heart, not brain-to-heart. It has to be genuine."

Codianni is one of those folks who just loves people. He loves buying them presents, he loves inviting them out on his boat, he loves to cook for them. Codianni has nineteen first cousins, and he's taken them all to Italy. Ask the people who work with him, and they'll tell you they love to be around him. He makes them feel good. Indeed, he is genuine.

But don't ever mistake Codianni's love of people for a willingness to forget about standards. Exemplary leadership is soft and demanding, caring and conscientious. As Codianni puts it, "I always tell trainers in my group that they have to master the program first, and then they're free to change it." To Codianni, having a clear set of expectations about what people will achieve is part and parcel of being caring.

When you were a kid, you probably read *Alice in Wonderland*. Remember the croquet match? The one where flamingos were the mallets, playing card soldiers were the wickets, and hedgehogs were the balls? Remember how in that match all the pieces kept moving and the rules kept changing all the time?

> "I don't think they play at all fairly," Alice began in a rather complaining tone, "and they all quarrel so dreadfully one can't hear oneself speak—and they don't seem to have any rules in particular; at least, if there are, nobody attends to them—and you've no idea how confusing it is all the things being alive. . . ."[1]

Poor Alice, she became so frustrated. There was no way of knowing how to play the game to win. There seemed no reason even to play the game. It was rigged in favor of the Queen of Hearts, anyway. And for the queen, that was really the point.

We've all been Alice at one time or another in our lives. We've been unsure where we're supposed to be going, what the ground rules are that govern how we behave, or how we're doing along the way. Just when we think we get the hang of it, the boss comes along and changes everything. This is a recipe for maddening frustration and pitiful performance. Our hearts just aren't in it.

The first prerequisite for encouraging the heart is to *set clear standards*. As we pointed out earlier, by *standards* we mean both goals and values (or principles). They both have to do with what's expected of us, but goals connote something shorter-term, whereas values and principles imply something more enduring. Typically, values and principles serve as the basis for goals; they define the arena in which goals and metrics must be set.

WE CAN LEARN A LOT FROM THE SCOUTS

We can learn a lot about leadership from the Girl Scouts and Boy Scouts. Both of us have had personal experience with these organizations, and we've experienced the power of clear standards and the role that recognition plays in honoring achievement.

In these organizations, boys and girls learn and pledge to uphold certain principles. They earn advancement and recognition from their deeds. As they achieve specific goals they earn merit badges, and if they earn enough merit badges they attain a defined rank. Recognition for achievement is a patch, a ribbon, a medal, a pin.

But the nice part about it is they get to wear them on their uniforms for all to see. Their peers know what they've accomplished and how they've earned it. It's probably no coincidence that people from scouting backgrounds, in proportion to their percentage of the general population, are more likely to serve in civilian leadership roles than people without that experience. The merit badges don't make the difference, of course; rather, it's the standards and the discipline. The badges are the symbols of living up to the standards.

We've often fantasized what it would be like if we had this same tradition in adult organizations. What if every time you achieve a standard you get a patch or a pin to wear that signals to everyone what you've done?

Actually, someone does that. As Kathy Johnson, manager of employee and organization development for Oak Ridge National Laboratory, explained to us, graduates of some of the lab's leadership development programs wanted to start a group to support their ongoing growth and development as they applied what they learned in the classroom to their jobs. With the enthusiastic endorsement and aid of Johnson and her colleagues, the graduates started the Oak Ridge National

Laboratory Leadership Action Consortium. By joining the now one-hundred-strong consortium, people commit not only to furthering their own development but also to taking on an action project that benefits the lab.

Dan McDonald, director of the instrumentation and control division and a person deeply committed to leadership development, volunteered to chair the consortium. To add extra meaning and uniqueness to this initiative, McDonald borrowed from his martial arts background and came up with the idea of "pin progression." McDonald defined seven levels of achievement for the Oak Ridge National Laboratory Leadership Action Consortium; just as colored belts in the martial arts serve to signify levels of mastery, colored pins serve that purpose in the consortium:

1. White is the first level. It signifies an *expression of interest* and a desire to develop yourself as a leader.
2. Orange, the second level, signifies the *beginning of the journey.* Earning it requires completing one program in the lab's "Leadership Alive" series.
3. Green signifies *growth.* To earn it, you have to finish a second class and complete a project initiative with workgroup-wide impact in which aspects of effective leadership are evident.
4. Blue, the fourth level, signifies *nourishment.* You have to complete a divisionwide project initiative in which leadership principles are demonstrated.
5. Brown signifies *a strong foundation.* To earn it, you have to finish three leadership development classes and complete a project initiative of labwide impact but limited scope. Effective leadership principles also have to be demonstrated in the project.
6. Red denotes *passion,* at which level you have to complete a project initiative of labwide impact and moderate scope. Effective leadership principles have to be demonstrated.

7. Black is the top level; it signifies *service* and requires completion of a project initiative of labwide impact and complex scope. You also have to be regarded by your peers as a leadership role model for the laboratory.

What McDonald, Johnson, and the consortium members have done is create a simple yet elegant way of connecting performance with rewards. They've defined each level and communicated what has to be done to attain it; if standards are met, people can then proudly wear their accomplishments—literally.

What's even more meaningful, says Johnson, is how McDonald presents the pins personally. He's a highly respected lab leader, and his personal involvement signals the importance of human development and individual initiative to the success of the Oak Ridge National Laboratory. It's not just the pins; it's also the person.

But how exactly do specific goals—the seven levels in this particular case—and values such as personal growth and service contribute to encouraging the heart? Sure, we know what they have to do with performance, but what part do standards play in uplifting people's spirits, imparting confidence, increasing optimism and hope, or offering personal support? Let's take a look.

COMMITMENT FLOWS FROM PERSONAL VALUES[2]

Human beings just don't put their hearts into something they don't believe in. We don't commit energy and intensity to something that's not a fit for us personally. Like wearing a pair of slacks that are too tight, it's darned uncomfortable, we look awkward, we feel embarrassed, and we can't move around very easily.

Our research shows that values make a difference in how people behave inside organizations and how they feel about themselves, their colleagues, and their leaders. We know that people expect their leaders to stand for something; that they expect them to have the courage of their convictions; and that credibility is the foundation of leadership. The first step toward credibility as a leader is clarifying personal values.[3]

But when, as researchers, we took a deeper look at the question of shared values—the congruence between personal and organizational values—we found something quite thought-provoking[4]: clarity of personal values is the force that really makes the difference in an individual's level of commitment to an organization.

Figure 4.1 shows some data we've gathered on how values clarity influences a person's commitment to the organization's goals and objectives. The four cells represent four degrees of clarity about personal and organizational values. The numbers in the cells indicate the extent of people's commitment to their organizations, measured on a 7-point scale with 1 being low and 7 being high.

The highest number—signifying the highest level of commitment to the organization—is just where we'd expect it to be: in the cell that indicates a high level of clarity about *both* personal and organizational values. Shared values do make a difference.

The lowest levels of commitment are in the two cells indicating low clarity about *personal* values; this is true even when we have a high degree of understanding of what the *organization* stands for. Finally, the second highest level of commitment is where there's high clarity about personal values but low clarity about organizational values. Though this surprised us initially, it makes sense because individuals most clear on personal values are better prepared to make choices based on principles, including whether the principles of the organization fit with their own personal principles.

	Low	High
High	4.87	6.26
Low	4.90	6.12

Clarity of organizational values (vertical axis)

Clarity of personal values

FIGURE 4.1.

Values Congruence and Individual Commitment. *Source:* Posner, B. Z., and Schmidt, W. H. "Values Congruence and Differences Between the Interplay of Personal and Organizational Value Systems." *Journal of Business Ethics,* 1992, *12*(2), 174.

Personal values matter most when it comes to making a commitment to an organization. Tony Codianni says that "different people are motivated by different things. I have to understand their core values." As authors Hal Zina Bennett and Susan J. Sparrow point out, "If we are primarily leading our lives according to other people's conditions, it is virtually guaranteed that we will not be giving our all. Because we'll not be working in a way that allows us to best access our personal resources and abilities, we will be producing at less than our optimal levels in our jobs . . . an important part of who we are simply is not engaged."[5]

Yet we don't always put this knowledge into practice. We all know organizations—perhaps even our own—that send a team of executives off on a retreat to create a corporate values statement. They return with credo in hand, print it on posters, laminate it on wallet cards, make videotapes about it, publish it in the annual report, hold training classes to orient people to it, and chisel it in stone in the headquarters lobby. Then they wait for commitment to soar. It doesn't. And it won't.

These efforts are probably a huge waste of time and money *unless* there's also a concerted effort to help individuals understand their own values and examine the fit between theirs and the organization's. We aren't suggesting for one second that organizational values are not important. But organizational values are only one side of the equation. Commitment is a matter of the fit between person and organization, and personal values drive fit.

The implication for leaders is that a unified voice on values results from discovery and dialogue. Leaders must engage individuals in a discussion of what the values mean and how their personal beliefs and behaviors are influenced by what the organization stands for. Leaders must also be prepared to discuss values and expectations in recruiting, selecting, and orienting new members. Better to explore early the fit between person and organization than to find out, late in some sleepless night, that we're in violent disagreement over matters of principle.

GOALS CONCENTRATE OUR MINDS AND SHAPE WHO WE ARE

Values set the stage for action. Goals release the energy.

University of Chicago professor Mihalyi Csikszentmihalyi has studied the state called "flow" for over two decades. Flow experiences are those times when we feel pure enjoyment and effortlessness in what we do. Among his findings, he reports that "in order to experience flow, it helps to have clear goals—not because it is achieving the goals that is necessarily important, but because without a goal it is difficult to concentrate and avoid distractions. Thus a mountain climber sets as her goal to reach the summit not because she has some deep desire to achieve it, but because the goal makes the experience of climbing possible. If it were not for the summit, the climb would become pointless ambling that leaves one restless and apathetic."[6]

Though many of us perceive goals as the finish line, Csikszentmihalyi is suggesting that the important function of goals is to get us moving with purpose and energy. What's really important to being our best is concentration and focus on something that is meaningful to us. By intending to do something, by setting a goal, we begin doing something. We take action. The action we take has an intent. It's not aimless wandering; there's a purpose to our actions. We're not just marking time; we understand why we're doing what we're doing.

Goals also help us concentrate our minds and block out annoying distractions. They keep our eye on the prize. Voice mail, e-mail, fax, phone calls, internal memos, pagers, and shouts over the cubicle wall disrupt our work constantly. How do we know what to respond to? How do we know what to say yes, or no, to? Goals and intentions keep us on track. They tell us to put the phone in do-not-disturb mode, close the door, and schedule our time.

Exemplary leaders make sure that work is not pointless ambling, but purposeful action. The very act helps people feel more alive, more in charge, more significant. Goal setting affirms the person, and whether we realize it or not it contributes to what people think about themselves. As Csikszentmihalyi points out, "It is the goals that we pursue that will shape and determine the kind of self that we are to become. . . . Without a consistent set of goals, it is difficult to develop a coherent self. . . . The goals one endorses also determine one's self-esteem."[7]

Is it better that individuals set their own goals, or should leaders set the goals for others? In the best of all worlds, people would set their own. Vast amounts of research give evidence that people feel best about themselves and what they do if they voluntarily do something. However, "people do not feel worst when what they do is obligatory"; they feel the worst, in fact, "when what they do is motivated by not having anything else to do."[8]

You can probably relate to this. Remember when you were given make-work? You had completed some task, and your manager couldn't figure out anything else for you to do, so he sent you to make photocopies to keep you busy. Idleness is the devil's workshop, and all that. Well, the net effect is a stack of papers and a person who feels like just a pair of hands at the boss's disposal. The lesson for leaders is to be sure people know why doing something is important, and what end it serves.

GOALS PLUS FEEDBACK KEEP US ENGAGED

People need to know whether they're making progress or marking time. Goals serve that function, but it's not enough simply to know that we want to make it to the summit. We need to know if we're still climbing, or if we're sliding downhill.

There is revealing research about the impact that clear and positive communication has on internal motivation and physical stamina. In one study, Stanford University's Albert Bandura wanted to find out how people's willingness to put forth effort to perform a task was influenced by the presence or absence of goals and feedback. He found that people's motivation to increase productivity on a task increases only when they have a challenging goal and receive feedback on their progress.[9] As shown in Figure 4.2, goals without feedback, and feedback without goals, have little effect on motivation.

Just announcing that we have a quality goal of zero defects is not enough to get people to put forth more effort. Goals alone are insufficient unless we get some information along the way about how we're doing. Similarly, just giving feedback has no net effect. People ask, "Zero defects? Why are you giving me feedback about that? I didn't know that was our goal!" But with clear goals and detailed feedback, people become self-corrective and more easily understand their place in the big picture.[10] With feedback, they can also determine what help they need from others and who might benefit from their assistance. Under these conditions, they're willing to put forth more productive effort.

A fascinating study involved soldiers who underwent several weeks of arduous training throughout which they were competing for places in special units.[11] At the end of training, one final challenge remained: a forced march in full gear. Motivation at the time of the march was extremely high among the recruits; they knew that failure to maintain the pace during the forced march meant losing the chance to join the special units.

For the march, the soldiers were divided into four groups. During the march, there would be no communication whatsoever between the groups. Each group would march twenty kilometers (about twelve and a half miles) over exactly the same terrain on the same day; the only variation was in the verbal instructions the groups received.

- The first group of soldiers were told the exact distance they would march—twenty kilometers—and they were regularly informed of their progress along the way.

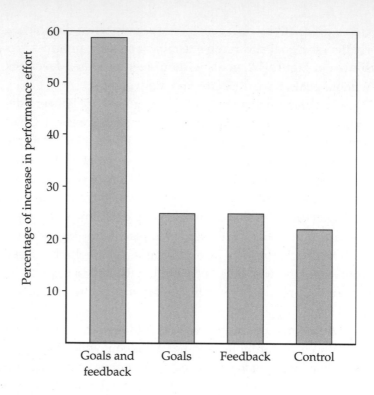

FIGURE 4.2.
How Goals and Feedback Affect Motivational (Performance)
Levels. *Source:* Bandura, A., and Cervone, D. "Self-Evaluation and
Self-Efficacy Mechanisms Governing the Motivational Effects of Goal
Systems." *Journal of Personality and Social Psychology,* 1983, *45,*
pp. 1017–1028.

- Group two soldiers were told only, "This is the long march you heard about." Nobody knew exactly how far they would march, nor were they informed of their progress along the way.
- Group three soldiers were told they would march fifteen kilometers. After marching fourteen kilometers, they were told they had six more to go.
- The fourth group of soldiers were told they would march twenty-five kilometers. After marching fourteen, they were told they had six more to go.

Upon completion of the march, the four groups were assessed to determine which one performed best and which endured the most stress. Which group do you think did the best and suffered the least from the stress of the march? Which group did the worst and suffered most?

Did you guess it? The researchers found that group one performed the best. Knowing how far they were going and getting regular reports were the keys to achieving the highest ratings.

As you might also expect, group two performed the worst. Knowing only that "this is the long march you've been waiting for," not knowing how far they were to march, and receiving no information along the way yielded poor results. Remember, these were soldiers in top condition who had completed the same training as group one. There was no difference in their group makeup. So the next time you hear something like, "Well this is the challenge we've all been waiting for," watch out. It's time to ask for some more information.

Surprising to some is that group three received the second highest rating. These were the soldiers who were told that they would march fifteen kilometers, but at fourteen kilometers they were told they had another six kilometers to go.

Apparently, for a highly motivated group this was not as much of a letdown as group four's condition.

Group four finished third. They were told they would march twenty-five kilometers but then at fourteen were told they had six more to go. Apparently, it's more of a letdown to think you have farther to go and then learn you have less, than to learn you have more. It appears to take the spring out of your step.

Blood tests for stress indicators were taken during the march and twenty-four hours later; the results corresponded with the discussion above. Specifically, blood was tested for cortisol and prolactin, hormones that rise with stress. Predictably, the highest levels were found in the group that knew the least about the march (group two). The lowest levels were found in the group that knew exactly how far they would be going and received regular progress reports (group one).

Results from the forced march, and similar studies, tell us of life-enhancing capacities. At the very least, if leaders provide a clear sense of direction and provide feedback along the way, they encourage people to reach inside and do their best. Leaders make the impossible possible and motivate people to strive to make the possible a reality. Information about goals and the progress toward those goals strongly influences not only our ability to achieve but also how well and how long we live. Talk about encouraging the heart!

ENCOURAGEMENT IS FEEDBACK

Encouragement, it can be said, is a form of feedback. It's positive information that tells us that we're making progress, we're on the right track, we're living up to the standards. But the wonderful thing about encouragement is that it's more personal than other forms of feedback. Encouragement requires us to get close to people, show that we care about them, and demonstrate that we are interested in others. Because it's more personal and positive, encouragement is more likely to accomplish something that other forms of feedback cannot. Encouraging the heart strengthens trust between leaders and constituents, a relationship that is absolutely critical to getting extraordinary things done in organizations.

Encouraging the heart accomplishes something else essential to excellence. It speaks to people's hearts—to deeply held values and beliefs, to something beyond the material—and contributes to creating meaning in the workplace.

There's a deep human yearning to make a difference. With books like M. Scott Peck's *The Road Less Traveled*[12] selling millions of copies, and staying on the bestseller lists not for weeks but for years, clearly people are searching for deeper meaning in their lives. People really do want to make commitments and unite in a common cause where they can accomplish extraordinary things. Great leaders, like great companies, create *meaning*, not just money.

The most admired leaders in every walk of life know that the first essential for enlisting others is to find and focus on the very best that the culture shares in common and what it means to the members. This communion of purpose helps bind us together. It joins us together in the human family. The best leaders are able to bring out and make use of this human longing for meaning and fulfillment. When leaders unequivocally communicate clear standards, they honor everyone's desire to do their very best. They elevate the human spirit.

But to ensure that people do in fact achieve their best, leaders have to bring forth the best from others. Bringing forth the best begins with belief, which then becomes a self-fulfilling prophecy.

- What values and principles do you most cherish?
- How do you communicate these beliefs to others?
- How clear are others about what you stand for?
- How are you creating meaning, and not just making money or motions?
- How clear and specific are the goals of those you're leading—clear and specific for you and for them?
- How do you, and how do they, know success when it happens? How do you and they see it, experience it, feel it?
- How are you getting feedback on how you're doing as a leader?
- How are others getting feedback on their performance?
- How useful is this feedback in helping you and others improve?
- How can you enhance the ways you and others get feedback?

CHAPTER FIVE

The Second Essential
Expect the Best

From the first day in school until the day I graduated, everyone gave
me one hundred plus in art. Well, where do you go in life? You go to
the place where you got one hundred plus.
— LOUISE NEVELSON, sculptor

I n Greek mythology, there is a story about a king of
Cyprus. Pygmalion is not only a king but also a sculptor. One day, he carves a statue of a beautiful young
woman. He falls in love with her image and is so enamored of
his creation that he spends all his time gazing at her and thinking about her. He longs to bring her to life but knows that, alas,
she is only made of ivory. Heartsick, the yearning Pygmalion
summons Aphrodite, the goddess of beauty, love, and fertility.
He pleads with her to bring his beautiful statue to life. Aphrodite grants the king his wish and gives the statue life. Pygmalion, of course, is overjoyed.

Based on this classic tale, playwright George Bernard
Shaw wrote *Pygmalion* for the stage. You may remember it as
the musical *My Fair Lady*. In it, Professor Henry Higgins, a
teacher of phonetics, meets an ill-spoken Cockney flower girl
named Eliza Doolittle. Higgins believes he can, by the force
of his skill and will, transform the flower girl into a lady. His

efforts and Doolittle's courage and persistence lead to her transformation. But the results are more than simply play acting. Not only does she learn to speak and act like a lady but Eliza Doolittle becomes one inside. She learns to believe in herself.

Social and behavioral scientists began to apply the lessons of this legendary story to classrooms and the workplace. Robert K. Merton, a professor of sociology at Columbia University, coined the phrase "self-fulfilling prophecy," theorizing that when a person predicts that something will occur, the expectation changes how the person behaves. The changed behaviors make the event more likely to happen.

Harvard professor Robert Rosenthal extensively tested this theory and coined the term "Pygmalion effect" in the course of one of his experiments to explain what occurred. He and co-researchers discovered that if we expect others to succeed, they probably will. If we expect them to fail, they probably will. People tend to live up, or down, to our expectations of them. Hundreds of research studies have since been conducted to test this notion, and they all clearly demonstrate that people tend to act consistently with our expectations.[1]

If we have someone in our life who believes in us, and who constantly reinforces that belief through her interactions with us, we are in fact strongly influenced by that support. If the potential exists within us, it comes out when a leader takes the time to bring us along. Indeed, observations show that managers communicate expectations in a number of ways. Managers with positive expectations set a climate that makes people feel more at ease. They offer positive reinforcement, give others information, give others opportunity for input and resources to do their jobs, and are likely to lend them assistance and give them better assignments. Those with negative expectations behave the opposite. Now, which set of behaviors do you think are likely to produce better results? The manager's attitude influences his or her behavior toward others, and the behavior influences the results.[2]

Even more important, researchers have found that as people learn they are capable of performing in particular ways, they begin to develop a self-expectation. Their own self-prophecies become self-fulfilling. Tom Melohn puts it this way: "Simply stated, people *must* believe that they are capable of solving the problem, of finding a new and better way. Or they won't. They can't if they don't believe in themselves, in their own capabilities. . . . Our coworkers can believe in themselves more if someone they respect is a fellow believer in them. That's what we tried to do at NATD, repeatedly reinforcing our associates' self-esteem, their competence, their capability."[3]

Common sense, right? No manager in her right mind would think or act differently, right? Not according to Jean-François Manzoni, professor of accounting and control, and Jean-Louis Barsoux, research fellow, at INSEAD, in Fontainebleau, France. Their meticulous research found that "bosses—albeit accidentally and usually with the best intentions—are often complicit in an employee's lack of success. How? By creating and reinforcing a dynamic that essentially sets up perceived under-performers to fail. . . ."[4]

In a reversal of the great-expectations dynamic of the Pygmalion effect, the set-up-to-fail syndrome can begin quite innocently, as Manzoni and Barsoux explain it. An employee seems to have a performance problem—a missed deadline, a lost account. Or it can start when a manager distances himself from a direct report for personal reasons. This triggers an increase in the manager's supervision and control of the direct report. The direct report then begins to believe that the manager lacks trust and confidence in her. Eventually, because of low expectations the direct report withdraws and stops making independent decisions or taking initiative. This, of course, reinforces the manager's original assessment that the individual is a poor performer, and the problem intensifies.

Manzoni and Barsoux observe that the set-up-to-fail syndrome "is self-fulfilling and self-reinforcing—it is the quintessential vicious circle. The process is self-fulfilling because the boss's actions contribute to the very behavior that is expected from weak performers. It is self-reinforcing because the boss's low expectations, in being fulfilled by his subordinates, trigger more of the same behavior on his part, which in turn triggers more of the same behavior on the part of the subordinate."[5]

High expectations or low expectations both influence other people's performance. Only high expectations have a positive impact on actions and on feelings about oneself. Only high expectations can encourage the heart.

HIGH EXPECTATIONS LEAD
TO HIGH PERFORMANCE

Successful leaders have high expectations, both of themselves and of their constituents. These expectations aren't just *fluff* that they hold in mind to keep a positive outlook or psych themselves up. Another person's belief in our abilities accomplishes much more than that. The expectations that successful leaders hold provide the framework into which people fit their own realities. As with Pygmalion, the framework plays an important role in developing people. Maybe you can't turn an ivory statue into a real person, but you can release the highest potential of your constituents.

Nancy Tivol, executive director of Sunnyvale Community

Services (SCS) in California, is a wonderful example of this principle in action. She believes strongly in her own ability and in those of every staff member and volunteer. When Tivol first arrived at SCS in 1991, volunteers were in her opinion underused. Many board members and paid staff felt that volunteers didn't have the skills to handle interactions with clients, donors, and corporate contacts. Tivol believed they could. Today, SCS has volunteers doing things that only staff members did previously. Indeed, more than seven hundred volunteers run the front office, the agency's three food programs, the Community Christmas Center, the agency's computer operations, and the Volunteer Language Bank—all under one director of volunteers. Most of the lead volunteers are over sixty-five years of age. Volunteer hours increased from six thousand to twenty thousand annually, which enabled paid staff to be reduced through attrition from twelve to eight FTE.

Not only that, but SCS became the county's only emergency assistance agency that has not turned eligible clients away because available funds were depleted. Under Tivol's leadership, SCS has increased its funding for the emergency assistance program for low-income families during a recession and a period in which many agencies experienced significant funding cutbacks! Six years ago, SCS distributed $34,000 to prevent evictions and utility disconnections, to pay for medical care and prescriptions; last year, SCS distributed $240,000. Six years ago, SCS helped 80 families a month with food; now it helps more than 525, and the grocery bags are much fuller.

Previous administrators, as well as paid staff, had made certain assumptions about volunteers. They assumed that because they were volunteers, they would be neither motivated enough nor skilled or experienced enough to take on the responsibility that some of the tasks at the agency would require.

As a result, volunteers were mostly employed at jobs that demanded very little of them, and they were given only minimal responsibilities. The bottom line was that they were never given the opportunity to explore or demonstrate their own capacities beyond the performance of the most menial tasks. Their beliefs, their *prophecies*, as it were, held the volunteers back; Tivol's beliefs encouraged the same group of people to excel. She placed volunteers in responsible positions, gave them the training and direction they required, and encouraged them to do their best. And they did just that!

When it became evident that SCS was going to need to upgrade its computer system, the assumption was that SCS didn't have the money to set up the new system and train people. Tivol saw this not as an obstacle but as an opportunity. Once again, she turned to volunteers—entrusting the job to her fifteen-year-old son, a computer whiz who found the prospect a real challenge. For his Eagle Scout project, he wrote a forty-one-page manual. Then he trained ten boy scouts from his troop to become "coaches," who in turn taught others in the agency how to use the new computer system. Each scout adopted a staff member or volunteer and stood by them as they learned the system.

What was the motivation that drove the volunteers? Why did the SCS picture so radically change under Tivol? The key was that she had very high *expectations* of her volunteers, and they literally breathed new life into the people around her. She prophesied their success.

Our own research shows that people are often anxious or nervous when they are encouraged by people in leadership positions to deliver their personal best. But in our surveys of people who experienced such challenges, with leaders holding high expectations for them, they marched in and did what was expected without hesitation. All those we interviewed were willing and excited by the challenges they faced. Spurred on by their leaders' high expectations, they developed self-confidence that gave them the courage and volition to live up to their leaders' expectations.

This demonstration of belief in another's abilities doesn't only come in organizational settings. It can show up anywhere. A moving and powerful instance came to us from Idaho businessman Don Bennett. Bennett was the first amputee to climb to the summit of Mt. Rainier. That's 14,410 feet, on one leg and two crutches!

During a difficult portion of the climb, Bennett and his team had to cross an ice field. To get across the ice, the climbers had to put crampons on their boots to prevent slipping and to dig into the ice for leverage and stability. Unfortunately, with only one cramponed boot and two crutches Bennett got stuck in the ice. The only way he could figure to get across the ice field was to fall face forward onto the ice, pull himself as far forward as he could, stand up, and then fall forward again. He was going to get across the ice field by falling down.

On this particular climb, his young teenage daughter happened to be with him, and she saw what was happening to her dad. While the team leader cut holes in the ice so Bennett could hop into the clear snow and traverse the ice field, Bennett's daughter stayed by his side through the entire four-hour struggle. As Bennett hopped, she shouted in his ear: "You can do it, Dad. You're the best dad in the world. You can do it, Dad!"

After Bennett told us this story, we knew there was no way he was *not* going to make it across that ice field with his daughter shouting that in his ear. You want to know what leadership is? What Kathy did is leadership. Her belief in her father and her verbal encouragement touched a place deep within Bennett, strengthening his resolve and commitment.

POSITIVE IMAGES CREATE
POSITIVE POSSIBILITIES

Positive expectations yield positive results. They also begin to create positive images in our minds, which yield other positive possibilities. Positive futures for self and others are first constructed in our minds. As Case Western Reserve University professor David Cooperrider puts it, "We see what our imaginative horizon allows us to see."[6] Seeing is believing, and the results can be life-affirming and life-enhancing.

Athletes have known for a long time that stored mental pictures influence performance. Unless we can see ourselves as being successful, it is very difficult to produce the behavior that leads to success. Experiment after experiment shows that positive images make groups more effective; relieve symptoms of illness; and enhance achievement in school, the military, and business.[7]

One intriguing experiment involving bowlers demonstrates the power of positive images on performance. Divided into different groups, sets of bowlers were first instructed in effective bowling methods. Following these lessons, the bowlers practiced. Some of those who practiced were videotaped. One group of the videotaped bowlers saw only the positive things they did, and the other group saw only the negative. Those who saw only their positive moves improved significantly more than any of the bowlers. Among unskilled bowlers, those who saw positive tapes improved their performance significantly more than anyone.[8]

Dutch sociologist Fred Polak has observed that "the rise and fall of images of the future precedes or accompanies the rise and fall of cultures. As long as a society's image is positive and flourishing, the flower of culture is in full bloom. Once the image begins to decay and lose its vitality, however, the culture does not long survive."[9] There is deep truth in what Polak says. Take a look around your organization, your community, your neighborhood. Are the images painted and the stories told positive, or negative? What does this portend? Is your organization's culture in ascendance, or in decay? Given the increasing cynicism of the workforce, one might legitimately wonder what the future holds. If what Polak says is true, as individuals and as leaders we had better begin to paint more affirmative images for ourselves and our constituents if we want to encourage others to commit to positive actions.

WHO LEADS THE LEADERS?

It's evident that just as leaders' high expectations can have a Pygmalion effect on their constituents, so the expectations of constituents can influence the behavior of their leaders. It has been shown that when constituents communicate high expectations of how good a person can be as a leader, the potential leader may adjust her self-concept and self-expectations to match what others think of her. With this motivation for exemplary leadership behavior, the constituents' prophecy is fulfilled.[10]

It is no wonder, then, that when people tell us about the leaders who really make a difference in their lives, they frequently tell us about people who believe in them and encourage them to reach beyond their own self-doubts, to more fully realize their own greatest strengths. They talk about leaders who treat them in ways that buoy their self-confidence, making it possible for them to achieve more than they themselves initially believe possible.

As a way to encourage the heart, the Pygmalion effect gets high ratings with successful leaders. In its simplest form, it can boost self-esteem. To speak metaphorically, it seeks and finds the beauty hidden in the stone. In fact, we might view increased self-esteem, produced by high expectations, as the fulcrum for leveraging change. Research as well as everyday experience confirm that people with high self-esteem, regardless of their age, level of education, or socioeconomic status "feel unique, competent, secure, empowered, and connected to the people around them."[11]

SELF-ESTEEM IS A WIN FOR ALL

To illustrate the power of self-esteem and self-fulfilling prophecies, social psychologists Robert Wood and Albert Bandura put together a very interesting experiment. They created a simulated organization and then brought in working professionals to manage it. These professionals were asked to match employee attributes with job requirements and then master a complex set of decision-making rules in how to guide and motivate their employees.

Half the professionals participating in this experiment were told that decision-making skills are developed through practice—that is, they are *acquired* skills. The other half were told that such skills reflect one's basic cognitive capacities, meaning they are *stable* skills. Thus, one group was working from the premise that decision making could be learned; the other was working from the premise that you either have these skills or you don't.

The two professional groups were then given management tasks that included motivating people participating in the simulation as employees. Throughout the simulation, the subjects were asked to rate their own effectiveness in getting the group they managed to perform at the desired productivity levels. In the beginning, both managerial groups expressed a moderately strong sense of managerial effectiveness. However, as they tried to get their employees to fulfill increasingly difficult production standards, the stable-skill group's self-ratings plummeted. Similarly, as their self-perceptions fell, their attitudes toward their employees became quite uncharitable; they began regarding their subordinates as incapable of being motivated, unworthy of supervision, and deserving termination.

Those managers in the acquired-skill group, who were getting exactly the same problems as the stable-skilled group, maintained a high level of perceived self-efficacy. Since they believed their abilities could be acquired, they set more challenging goals and made excellent use of analytical strategies. They believed they could learn, so they did. The conviction influenced their belief in and behavior toward others.

In real life, Antonio Zarate demonstrated the power of this principle. He led the turnaround of Metalsa, an automotive metal stamping company in Monterrey, Mexico, from one with a 10 percent rejection rate and only a domestic market into an award-winning, world-class business with 40 percent exports. He accomplished all this with the same local Mexican workforce that was staffing Metalsa when he took on the challenge. The difference was that Zarate believed the workers could do it. He believed that there are no poor-quality workers, only *underled companies*. He never gave up on his workers—and he never gave up on himself.

What do we learn from all this? Clearly, before we can encourage the heart, we have to believe in others, and in ourselves. Our belief in others has positive benefits for individual leaders, for their constituents, and for the organizations they serve. High expectations matter—a lot.

The thoughts and beliefs we hold in our minds are intangible. They can't be weighed and measured like the raw materials that come in and the finished products that run off the assembly line. But seen or not, measurable or not, they have an enormous impact on the people around us. Exemplary leaders know this and know how to purposefully hold in their minds high expectations for themselves and other people.

With the attitude that people live up to high expectations, and with clear standards, leaders have to pay attention to what's happening around them so they can find positive examples to recognize. In the next chapter, we take a look at what it means to really pay attention to what's going on around you.

REFLECTING ON
EXPECTING THE BEST

- How would you honestly rate your expectations of those you lead? High? Moderate? Low?
- Think about some of the lower performers among those you lead. How might your expectations be influencing their performance? What behaviors can you identify that might be contributing to disappointing performance?
- Think about your high performers. How might your expectations be influencing their performance? What behaviors can you identify that might be contributing?
- What does this assessment tell you?
- What images of the future do you hold in your mind right now? Would you say they are mostly positive, or mostly negative?
- How are you communicating these images of the future right now? How are they influencing others?
- What's your opinion about whether the people you lead can learn the skills required to do their jobs? Can they acquire them, or are they mostly innate?
- Right now, how do you communicate positive expectations of others?

CHAPTER SIX

The Third Essential
Pay Attention

Creative leaders find ways of stepping into the shoes of other people
and asking, "How would I feel and what would I want if I were this
person?"

—GAY HENDRICKS and KATE LUDEMAN, *The Corporate Mystic*

eaders are out and about all the time. They're not in
their offices much; the demands of the job keep them
mobile. They're attending meetings, visiting customers, touring the plants or service centers, dropping in on the
lab, making presentations at association gatherings, recruiting
at local universities, holding roundtable discussions, speaking
to analysts, or just dropping by employee's cubicles to say
hello. It's the nature of leaders to wander; it goes with the territory. In fact, at its root the word *lead* comes for an Old English
word that means "go, travel, guide."

None of these wanderings should be purposeless. Leadership is not a stroll in the park; leaders are out there for a reason.
One of the reasons, we maintain, is to show that they care. Recall from Chapter Two that Tom Melohn called it CBWA, caring by walking around. One way of showing you care is to *pay
attention* to people, to what they're doing, and to how they're
feeling. If you are clear about the standards of behavior you're
looking for and you believe and expect that people will perform

like winners, then you're going to notice lots of examples of people doing things right, and doing the right things.

Paying attention is all about being curious, really. Remember in the NATD case how Melohn *saw* Kelly put the part in the freezer. There he was, caring by wandering around, and he noticed something. But just noticing is not sufficient to encourage the heart, so he went up to Kelly and started to ask him some questions. He showed an interest in him. He wanted to know more, not because he wanted to check up on Kelly but because he was *curious*.

We've noticed something in all the years we've been doing leadership research. The vast majority of people are willing to talk about themselves, especially when they're talking about the best things they've done. But you won't learn about it unless you're curious, unless you look for it, unless you pay attention. Your curiosity shows you care.

Now, we don't know too many leaders who set out on daily tours exclusively to search for people doing things. The reality is that most leaders don't just go out scouting for exemplars. They don't have to, though. To be effective, you don't have to write in your daily planner *Go out and find someone who is behaving consistently with our values and goals so I can reward and recognize them at our weekly meeting*. It'd be great if you could do it, and maybe you should. After all, Melohn found time. But the point is that whenever and wherever you're walking around, you must really pay attention to people and actively search for positive examples.

DITCH THE SHINY BADGE

In their book *Managing from the Heart*, authors Hyler Bracey, Jack Rosenblum, Aubrey Sanford, and Roy Trueblood tell the story of Harry Hartwell, the manager of an oil refinery in the southern United States. The refinery was his life. Hartwell would conduct daily inspection tours at the refinery. When he came around, conversations would stop, people would pick up the pace, and they'd really focus on their work. To him, inspections were an effective way to make sure production remained high and problems got identified.

But something else was actually going on. As the authors tell it, Hartwell "pictured himself conducting his next inspection tour dressed in Western attire and riding around on a horse, with a silver badge on his shirt. . . ."[1] He saw himself as dispensing "frontier justice." But even to Hartwell, the law-enforcer image was not funny; in fact, it was quite exhausting. All was not well with the sheriff with the shiny badge. Hartwell suffered a heart attack.

Hartwell's story is fictional, and it does have a happy ending. But the authors make an important point with this tale. Seeing oneself as a sheriff dispensing frontier justice is not the kind of self-image that ultimately leads to good health or healthy performance. But it is a perception many people have of managers.

As we saw in the last chapter, how we view ourselves and others influences our behavior, and our behavior influences others' behavior. Imagine what behaviors would follow if you saw yourself as a frontier sheriff with a shiny tin badge. Inspecting, controlling, checking up on others, finding fault with what they do, and looking for trouble are the kinds of action likely to flow from that self-image.

What happens in organizations where managers are constantly on the lookout for problems? Three things. First, they get a distorted view of reality. Second, over time production declines. Third, the manager's personal credibility hits bottom.

Put yourself in the worker's situation. If you knew someone was coming around to check up on you, how would you behave? As soon as you spot the boss coming, you put on your best behavior. Actually, we may put on *different* behavior, but it's not our *best*. In fact, it can be our worst. Why? Because we get nervous and tense, and when we're nervous and tense we slip up more. The manager who wanders around with an eye out for trouble is more likely to get just that: more trouble.

When we know that people are coming around to look for problems, we're more likely to hide them than reveal them—precisely the opposite effect of what is wanted. People who work for controlling managers are likely to keep information to themselves, not reveal the truth, and not be honest about what's going on. It's understandable; they know that little good comes from telling the truth.

This is why controlling managers have low credibility. Think about it. Why do people who exhibit highly controlling behaviors—inspecting, correcting, checking up, watching over, wanting to see work before it goes out—have low personal credibility? Because these behaviors signal that the manager does not trust you. If he trusted you, he wouldn't need to check up on you or approve every initiative. How do you respond to someone who doesn't trust you? You don't trust him. And since trustworthiness is a key element of personal credibility, credibility is diminished. We're much less likely to believe someone who doesn't exhibit trust in us.[2]

So, the first thing we've got to do when we're walking around our organizations is to ditch that shiny sheriff's badge. Instead, we've got to put on our Pygmalion glasses and expect to find the best.

RELEASE THE POSITIVE

It's only human nature that if we feel we're being watched by someone looking for our faults, we act very differently than we do in a supportive environment where we know there's an opportunity to be rewarded for special achievement. If we know someone is looking for positive examples, we make an effort to reveal them. The right things are there for others to notice.

If you see yourself as a caring leader, you act differently than when you see yourself as a controller. You express joy in seeing others succeed, you cheer others along, and you offer supportive coaching, rather than being a militant authority figure who is out patrolling the neighborhood.

As you take on the role of caring leader, people soon begin relating to you differently. They get the message that you're not out looking for ways to catch them screwing up but are instead looking for the opposite. In this environment, people open up. They no longer dread seeing you coming down the aisle.

If people know there's a caring leader in their midst, patrolling the organization in search of achievements to celebrate, it only stands to reason that they'll be stimulated to show you something you can honor and celebrate. They relax and want to offer the best of themselves. This positive focus on behavior and performance, linked to goals and values, significantly improves morale as it moves the company toward higher levels of performance and increased productivity.

In a supportive climate, people are also much more likely to help each other succeed. They teach and coach each other—another boost to productivity. In addition, in this open environment people are more likely to let you know when problems are brewing and lend a hand in solving them before they escalate.

When we asked Ted Avery, at the time general manager for the Houghton Winery in Western Australia, to describe his personal best leadership experience, one of the things he told us was this: "I would see great things that were going on in marketing, for example, and I'd tell them, 'Way to go!' I'd hear about a new development in operations and I'd go into the plant and tell them, 'Fantastic!' If they figured out a more efficient process in the fields, I'd go out and find those responsible and let them know how much we appreciated their hard work." That's what caring leaders do, and that's one of the reasons why, for Avery, it was a *personal best* leadership experience.

PUT OTHERS FIRST

Paying attention demands that you put others first. A recent study by Gregory Boyer confirms that the best leaders put others at the center of the universe.[3] In highly competitive, rapidly changing environments, caring and appreciative leaders are the ones to bet on for long-term success.

As mentioned earlier, for more than two decades we've been involved in systematic research, conducted in the public and private sectors, about managers' values and strategies for aligning personal and organizational values.[4] Our intention has been to take a broad look at managerial values because they are such a powerful force in organizational life. Values are at the core of our character, influencing the choices we make, the people we trust, the appeals to which we respond, and how we invest our time and energy.

Our research clearly shows a shift in some critical managerial values since our first study in 1980. Three values are most relevant to our discussion here. We've noticed that, compared to 1980, cooperative values are increasingly emphasized, focus is shifting from self to others, and home and family interests are receiving greater attention. At the same time, the managerial value statement that customers are the organization's key stakeholders has remained constant.

Looking out for number one—the mantra of the 1980s—is no longer what thinking managers think. Greater attention is now on others in the organization, rather than being directed toward personal needs. Will this hold true for the next generation of managers, those from the so-called Generation X? We're encouraged by the recent poll of America's youth (ages eighteen to thirty) conducted by Public Allies.[5] The survey indicates that young people have a cooperative view of problem solving (sharing responsibility for making decisions and moving forward) and a strong belief that leadership can be found among ordinary people in the community regardless of their positions or levels of authority. Young people also say that average people have the resources and practical know-how to solve most of the problems in their community rather than relying on experts to solve them. The most important leadership quality, say these young people, is "being able to see a situation from someone else's point of view." They're right because focusing on others is precisely what's required if we are to engender trust.

LISTEN WITH YOUR EYES AND YOUR HEART

Central to putting others first is the capacity to walk in their shoes. Learning to understand and see things from another's perspective is absolutely crucial to building trusting relations and to career success.[6] For example, studies from the Center for Creative Leadership reveal that successful executives derailed because of insensitivity and inability to understand the perspectives of other people. They undervalued the contributions of others, making them feel inadequate. They listened poorly, acted dictatorially, played favorites, and failed to give—or sometimes even share—credit with others. The net result over time was that these traits and attitudes caught up with them. When these managers really needed the help of others around them, they were left to fend for themselves, ignored, isolated, and on occasion purposely sabotaged.[7]

Listening is a crucial leadership skill. But not just any kind of listening.

A while back, we were attending the annual fundraising breakfast for the Opportunities Industrialization Center West, an extraordinary nonprofit job training and placement organization located in Menlo Park, California. One of the speakers that particular morning was Michael Pritchard, a well-known local comedian by night and a San Francisco probation officer by day. He loves kids, and he loves making people laugh.

Pritchard told a true story that we'll never forget. He was visiting a grade school and got to talking with a third grader. He asked her what she'd been learning, and she said sign language.

Pritchard was, as we were, intrigued by her response. Sign language? Kids don't typically learn sign language in third grade. So Pritchard asked how she got started on that educational adventure.

The young girl explained that her best friend since first grade couldn't speak and couldn't hear. So she asked her mom if she could learn sign language so she could communicate with her grade school friend. Her mom said yes and began to drive her daughter back and forth to lessons.

"Now," the young girl said, "I listen with my eyes and my heart, not just my ears and my brain." Wow! What a lesson that is.

All leaders can learn from this third grader. Listening with our eyes and hearts, not just our ears and brains, requires a deeper level of paying attention. It requires that we listen for understanding and not only for the words, that we hear the heart and see the soul. It's the only kind of listening that truly creates a capacity to encourage the heart.

Professors Suresh Srivastva and Frank Barrett of Case Western Reserve University underscore this point about listening in their writings on executive integrity. They note that it's "not the content of the exchange that is central but the experience of being taken in and heard, which not only affirms the legitimacy of one's way of looking at the world but then allows one to begin letting go of some defensiveness because the experience of affirmation increases one's capacity to affirm others."[8] As basic as this might seem, listening is not all that universal. Research by the Hay Group, covering one million employees in more than two thousand organizations, reveals that only about one in three people respond favorably to questions about how well their company listens to them.[9]

Eyes-and-heart listening can't be from a distance, reading reports or hearing things secondhand. Our constituents want to know who we are, how we feel, and whether we really care. They want to see us in living color. Since proximity is the best predictor of whether two people will talk to one another, you have to get close to people if you're going to communicate. Because most of our constituents can't come to us, we have to go to them. This means regularly walking the office hallways and plant floors; meeting often with small groups; and hitting the road for frequent visits with associates, key suppliers, and customers. It may even mean learning another language if a large portion of your workforce or customer base speak it.

What's so wonderful about the third-grade girl in Michael Pritchard's story is that she learned the language of another to strengthen their relationship. You might say, "Well that's because she had to, if she wanted to be her friend." Precisely! She had to learn sign language if she wanted to be a friend. Learning another's language, literally or figuratively, is essential to caring leadership. It's only by learning what others value, what they enjoy and treasure, that we can expect to reach their hearts.

When you're out there paying attention to the positive, you're highly visible, and you also make yourself known to others. While you're getting to know them, they're getting to know you. Who do you trust more, someone you know or someone you don't know?

Whenever we ask people this question, the universal answer is, "Someone I know." Of course, there may be people you know that you don't trust at all, but in general we're much more likely to trust friends than strangers. So a side benefit of actively appreciating others is that it increases their trust in you. This kind of relationship is more critical than ever as our workforce becomes more global and diverse. If others know we genuinely care about them, they're more likely to care about us. This is how we bridge cultural divides.

HANG OUT

Gretchen Kaffer, a human resource administrator with Honeywell-Measurex, learned the value of listening and being physically present when her department recently went through a reorganization. She used to spend time in the cafeteria and on the patio chatting with her coworkers during lunch hour, but she'd gotten too busy. With the reorganization, Kaffer's group moved into a refurbished building with a spacious new break room where four to five people could gather comfortably. Kaffer began to notice that since the move, people began to hang out in the break room for lunch. So she decided to make lunch a regularly scheduled part of her day and join her colleagues.

"The first couple of times I popped in," she reports, "everyone looked up at me as if I was coming to ask someone a work-related question. They were surprised that I was joining them for lunch. I think some people may have thought that I didn't want to spend time with them, since I had not in so long."

Kaffer likes to know what's going on with her coworkers. She likes "to be sensitive and approach people in a manner in which I think they'll be most receptive," but her absence created some distance. It didn't take long before Kaffer started to learn all sorts of things about her colleagues that she'd missed.

"It also opened up some good conversations about work and nonwork-related issues and events," she says. "It has really allowed us to hash over some changes and procedures that we wouldn't normally get to discuss in such a large group, because we rarely have time to discuss even the big stuff in groups of more than two or three. I think this has allowed my coworkers access to what I am doing. It gives them the opportunity to ask me questions, make suggestions, and fill me in on the not-so-important, but interesting and possibly telling, employee relations and interactions that I have been missing while cooped up in my office."

There was another benefit to the "lunch club thing," as they call it. Employees "from other departments seem pleasantly surprised by the laughter coming out of our break room. They walk by, or purposely seek us out, and sometimes they stop and ask if we're having a party. We often invite them to join us. . . . I think this has definitely improved our image as a team, given us greater visibility, and allowed us more contact with other employees in our building."

Since the gang's gotten used to Kaffer hanging out with them, they now expect to see her. "Around 12:00 or 12:15, there's usually a face in my doorway asking if I'm 'doing the lunch club thing.'"

Whether it's joining the lunch club or walking the plant floor, being present and paying attention to the concerns and accomplishments of others allows leaders to gather critical information. Some of this information is valuable in solving problems and some in recognizing contributions. The message from Kaffer is that you've got to be there to gather it. Funny thing: when you begin to hang out with folks and they know you're interested in them, they *want* to see you. Other people notice as well, and they want to join in too. People just like to be where people are enjoying themselves, even—or should we say, especially—at work.

BE A FRIEND AND OPEN UP

Managerial myth says we can't get too close to our associates. We can't be friends with people at work. Well, set this myth aside. Over a five-year period, professors Karen Jehn of the University of Pennsylvania's Wharton School, and Pri Pradhan Shah of the Carlson School of Management at the University of Minnesota, conducted studies in which they observed groups of friends and groups of acquaintances—people who knew each other only vaguely—performing motor-skill and decision-making tasks in two different situations. In one, the groups built models out of Tinkertoys. In the other, they ranked actual MBA candidates against given criteria. The groups' decisions were compared to those of the real admissions committee. "The results were unequivocal," Jehn and Shah report. "The groups composed of friends completed an average of 9 Tinkertoy models compared with the acquaintances' average of 2.45. As for decision making, the friends accurately matched an average of 3.1 of a possible 5 of the admissions committee's decisions, whereas the acquaintances averaged 2.44 matches."[10]

Jehn and Shah offer one important condition for interpreting these results, however. They find that friends have to be strongly committed to the group's goals. If not, then friends may not do better. This is precisely why we said earlier that it is absolutely necessary for leaders to be clear about standards and create a condition of shared goals and values. When it comes to performance, commitment to standards and good relations between people go together.

There's also strong evidence that we listen more intently to a person we perceive as a friend—someone who cares about us—than we do to a person we perceive only as a professional associate. Friends and family members are always our most important sources when it comes to information about health care, restaurants, where to go on a vacation, or what kind of new car to buy. Similarly, leaders who get out there and let themselves be known are much more likely to be accepted as members of the "family" than those who don't.

People are just more willing to follow someone they like and trust. To become fully trusted, we must be open—to others, but also *with* others. An open door is a physical demonstration of a willingness to let others in. So is an open heart. This means disclosing things about yourself. We don't mean the tabloidlike disclosures that seem to haunt leaders today. We mean talking openly about your hopes and dreams, your family and friends, your interests and your pursuits. We encourage you to tell others the same things you'd like to know about them.

When we're open, we make ourselves vulnerable. But this vulnerability makes us more human and more trusted. If neither person in a relationship takes the risk of trusting, at least a little, the relationship remains stalled at the lowly level of caution and suspicion. If leaders want the higher levels of performance that come with trust and collaboration, then they must demonstrate their trust *in* others before asking for trust *from* others. When it comes to trust, leaders ante up first.

Disclosing information about ourselves can be risky.[11] We can't be certain that other people will like us, appreciate our candor, agree with our aspirations, buy into our plans, or interpret our words and actions in the way we intend. But by demonstrating willingness to take such risks, leaders encourage others to reciprocate. Once the leader takes the risk of being open, others are more likely to take a similar risk—and thereby take the first steps necessary to build interpersonal trust.

Disclosing information about yourself is one way to be open. Asking for constructive feedback is another—not merely giving feedback to others, but asking for it yourself. When you're out there attending to what's happening, noticing the positive contributions people are making, stop and ask them for feedback. It's a demonstration that you appreciate them. By being open to influence, leaders encourage people to provide more information.[12]

"How am I doing?" might not initially seem like something a leader would ask, but it is a practice of the best leaders. Soliciting feedback is the reciprocal side of showing appreciation. Recognizing another's contribution is your gift to others. Feedback is their gift to you. It's a gift of information that enables you to grow and improve.

SEEK AND YE SHALL FIND

When you really pay attention—when you're curious, when you look for the best, when you put others first, when you listen with eyes and heart, when you hang out, when you open up to and with others—then you find what you're seeking. You notice all kinds of examples of people living up to and exceeding the standards that have been set. You find lots of opportunities to recognize individuals for their contributions.

REFLECTING ON
PAYING ATTENTION

- How often are you out there caring by wandering around?
- How do you show your curiosity?
- When you're out there, what do you pay attention to? What do you notice?
- Would you say you more often notice positive or negative things?
- To what extent does your behavior say, "I'm here looking for people doing things right and doing the right things?"
- To what extent does your behavior say, "I'm checking up on you"? Or, "I'm looking for problems"?
- How, specifically, do you pay attention to the positive?
- What forums do you use for listening?
- How well do your associates really know you? What have you told them about your hopes, dreams, joys, passions, life?
- What do you know about their hopes and dreams?
- How many of your colleagues would introduce you as their "friend"?
- How do you ask for feedback?
- Who, right now, in your organization, exemplifies the standards that have been set?
- When was the last time you talked to that person—or any person—about his or her work?
- When was the last time you recognized someone for his or her actions?

CHAPTER SEVEN

The Fourth Essential
Personalize Recognition

What I have discovered is that as I do the work of personalizing recognitions into the work of my team, I become a more empathic and involved leader in the process.

—CLAIRE JENKINS, Macrovision Corporation

Not too long ago, one of our colleagues, Steve Farber, received a thank-you note. As an extremely accomplished trainer and presenter, he gets a lot of thank-you notes. But this one was special.

The first thing that makes this thank-you note unique is that it was sent to Steve but addressed to Steve's son. Here's the letter verbatim.

To Steve's Son,

I understand that you're curious about what your dad does when his job takes him away from home. I'll bet it's tough on you sometimes to have him away when you'd like to have him home more than he is. As one of his students this past week, I thought you might like to know what he did to help me and others in the class that he taught.

Your dad has a lot of valuable knowledge about how businesses work and how to make them work better. Even more importantly, he helps people to make their lives better and happier. And he teaches all this in a fun way so that the time we spend with him in class is really enjoyable.

I just wanted you to know that we really appreciate your sharing him this week, and if he's anywhere near as good or as fun as a father as he is as a teacher, you've got yourself one fine dad.

Carl English
One of your dad's students

This simple thank-you note is an extraordinary example of how someone can turn something so commonplace into a unique event. Carl English, vice president of electric transmission and distribution at Consumers Energy in Jackson, Michigan, *personalized* his recognition. He could have purchased a preprinted thank-you card and then written a perfunctory note inside to Farber about how much he enjoyed being in the class. But he didn't.

English paid attention. He took the time to learn that Farber had a son who was curious about what his dad did at work. He wrote the note to the son, praising his dad for an exemplary job. This extra little effort—that's all it took—made the note something that Farber treasures and loves to share with others. Says Farber, "It made a huge difference. As much as I love my work, particularly on those days when I'd rather be at home than out on the road somewhere I think of that note, and it reminds me of why I go to work every day."

When Farber shared this note with folks at Consumers Energy, nobody there expressed surprise. English is known for the personal notes that he writes to people. If you really care about others, you pay attention to them. You find something special to say. It's easy. It becomes a habit. Even if this is the one hundredth or one thousandth note that English wrote, to Farber it's special because it's about *him* and his son.

So, who says business isn't personal? Business *is* personal, if you want to make it that way.

RECOGNITION CAN HURT
IF IT'S NOT PERSONALIZED

To truly recognize a person so that she's encouraged by your efforts, you absolutely have to know something about who she is—some of her likes and dislikes, whether she enjoys public recognition or shirks from it, and even what she is or is not willing to take credit for. We learned that in the last chapter. Failure to learn something about others can result in an act of recognition that has no meaning. In fact, it can even hurt.

Another colleague, Rebecca Morgan, an author, speaker, and managing partner of the Morgan Seminar Group in San Jose, California, told us a poignant story about a time when a well-meaning act of recognition boomeranged. It's an example of what *not* to do.

Morgan is a person who likes recognition that is "either one-to-one with me or in front of a group that is significant to me, that is sincere, shows appreciation, and is directed to my specific contributions and the effect they had on the project." Unfortunately, in the case she related to us, this did not happen. She tells it this way:

> The president of one of my professional associations once brought me and a handful of volunteers on stage at the end of a convention where I had served as logistics chair. I expected, perhaps, a few sentences about the two years I'd served on the committee preparing for the event, the two cross-country flights I'd made at my own expense for committee meetings, the hundreds of hours I'd put in, and the one hundred volunteers I'd recruited and trained.

Instead, he said two sentences I'll never forget: "Rebecca did the little things. If no one else would do it, we knew Rebecca would." I was stunned, crushed. It sounded like I'd collated a few packages, or made some copies. I could barely see my sixteen hundred colleagues giving us a standing ovation. When I got off stage, I had to leave the room. I cried for an hour. He had meant well; he just didn't think about it until we were on stage. Now, I know that when I acknowledge someone—I need to be clear on "How can I phrase this, to leave the person feeling honored, not diminished?"

Honored and not diminished. That's how we all want to feel. We can only genuinely honor someone when we know who she is, what she likes, and what she's done. We have to have the person in mind. Right now, I'm honoring Steve. How can I make this special for him? And now I'm honoring Rebecca; what can I do to make this special for her? But it's not enough to *know*; we also must *communicate* that we know.

KNOW WHAT THEY LIKE

David Bonilla, president of Advantage Business Solutions and a university administrator, told us another story that drives this point home. Bonilla's wife left her job as administrative secretary for a local church. At a Sunday morning worship, the staff recognized her seventeen-year service to the group by presenting her with a silver jewelry dish. Although the gift was generous in one respect, it fell far short of the goal of giving meaningful recognition because nobody asked Bonilla or his wife what she might like. It just so happened that she had never liked silver!

"Instead of being impressed or feeling appreciated," Bonilla told us, "she felt more ignored, discouraged, and resentful. So the moral of this story," he went on, "reinforces an old concept I heard somewhere. A manager should ask employees how they would like to be recognized. All of us are driven by different motivations—some slightly different, some greatly different."

As we were doing our research, Bonilla's story sparked a vigorous debate among an online chat group that was exchanging ideas with us on this subject. Most thought asking before giving was quite appropriate, but others thought asking before giving spoiled the surprise and took away from the basic intent.

We'll let you decide for yourself on this issue, but to us Bonilla's lesson seems sound. Better to ask someone what they'd like to receive if you don't really know than to create resentment from an otherwise gracious gesture. A leader who's out there scouting regularly can learn a person's likes and dislikes from friends, coworkers, family members, and direct observation. Most of the time, it should never be necessary to ask the recipient directly. After all, don't you explore what members of your family would like to receive when you're getting ready for that special occasion? What's getting in the way of doing that with colleagues at work?

Michael Levick, the director of consulting and education services for WBT Systems, put it this way to our chat group: "A good manager doesn't need to ask the employee what type of recognition she wants. A good manager knows the tastes and interests of her staff, because a good manager knows that showing an interest is the first and most important form of recognition. A good manager also learns from many small, casual acts of recognition what works for each staff member."

Ann Cessaris of Key Communication reminds us all of another reason why it's essential to personalize, or should we say "culturalize," recognition. "I had a client," she reported, "who was born in Asia, came to this country at age twelve, and was very well acclimated to life in the United States. However, when his boss rewarded his exceptional contribution to a team project by giving him a delightful corner office, he was horrified. He felt it destroyed the feeling of teamwork and his future relations with his team members."

"Cultural values run deep," says Cessaris, and she's absolutely correct. Personalizing is about knowing the other so well that you know what's appropriate individually or culturally. It's pretty arrogant for someone to assume that just because he's the leader he naturally knows what's right for others without even bothering to inquire or observe.

One of the most meaningful expressions of appreciation Jim Kouzes ever received was from a Japanese colleague, Hiroshi Watanabe. He was paying a visit to talk about his own investigations of leadership in Japan and wanted to chat about what he had learned and how it compared to our work. He visited Kouzes at his office; the meeting began, as is often the tradition, with an exchange of gratitude for the other. Watanabe took from his briefcase a small thank-you gift: a beautiful card affixed with an intricate and colorful Japanese kimono that had been handmade by Watanabe's wife. Then he presented Kouzes with another. It was a spectacular traditional Japanese scarf that had been handwoven by his mother. Watanabe said that when his mother learned that he was coming here, she wanted to participate, so she made the scarf for Kouzes's wife.

This event occurred during the time we were writing this book, and it was an important lesson in how important culture and person are to showing appreciation for another. Watanabe and his entire family got involved in the visit, something that is quite traditionally Japanese. They spent hours of personal labor and caring for a few moments of recognition. The visit, the person, and the family will never be forgotten. The handmade scarf and card are reminders forever of the power of getting personally involved in the life of another, and in a way that expresses the character of the culture.

THINK ABOUT IT

What it comes down to is *thoughtfulness*: how much effort you put into thinking about the other person and what makes the recognition special for that person. It means observing an individual and asking: "What would really make this special and unique for this person—make it a memorable, one-of-a-kind experience? What could I do to make sure that she never forgets how much she means to us? What can I do to make sure he always remembers how important his contributions are?"

This kind of thoughtfulness was evident in a story told to us by one of our former graduate students, Karen Bennett, the spouse of the founder of Glenn Valley Homes, a unique start-up company that builds computer-designed, precision-crafted custom homes in a plant in Orland, a small town north of Sacramento.

Thanks to the early success of this start-up, the new factory was faced with a backlog of home orders. President Wayne Bennett needed a highly skilled production manager to meet the extraordinary challenge they faced. From the pool of candidates, he selected Ray Freer, a veteran with fifteen years in the industry. Freer was an energetic worker, but one whose talents and expertise had not been fully used in previous jobs. He was anxious for the opportunity to demonstrate his skills and abilities in setting up and running a factory, even though he was quite aware that the time and financial pressures were huge. Bennett believed in Freer and entrusted him with full responsibility to lead the crew.

Bennett's confidence in Freer was well placed. After several six- and seven-day weeks, they were ready to begin regular production. The plant was state-of-the art, the previously inexperienced crew well trained, and Freer had personally built and installed additional buffer stations to augment production during unexpected delays. The first house was successfully cut, sized, and shipped within three days of the start of production. Here's how Karen Bennett tells what was done to let Freer know that his efforts had made a difference.

> To acknowledge Ray's extraordinary accomplishment at the first president's barbecue, Wayne called the group over to one side of the factory and asked Ray to demonstrate how one of the buffer stations worked. When Ray threw the lever to operate the skate-wheel conveyor that he had personally designed and constructed, a spring-loaded rod was unexpectedly released, displaying a flag with an envelope attached. When Ray looked inside the envelope, he found a five hundred dollar check and a letter from Wayne thanking him for his outstanding work. Wayne then read the letter out loud to the group, acknowledging the importance of Ray's creativity and hard work in preparing the production area in time to meet the first influx of home orders. Ray was clearly moved by Wayne's public display of appreciation, and the loud clapping and cheers of Ray's coworkers and crew clearly demonstrated their mutual support for his well-earned award.

Wayne Bennett obviously put some *thought* into this recognition. Like Melohn in our earlier case, he closely observed what Freer had done to contribute to the success of the factory, and he actually used equipment that Freer had personally constructed as an integral part of the celebration. Bennett then read aloud a personal note he'd written Freer, telling of his innovativeness, dedication, and tireless work on behalf of Glenn Valley Homes. A check always helps, and the boss can always hand it to the employee in private without all the rest of the ceremony. But not Wayne Bennett. He knew that personalizing recognition and telling the story in public would create more meaning.

REFLECTING ON
PERSONALIZING RECOGNITION

- What do you know about each of your key constituents: direct reports, peers you regularly interact with, key clients, important vendors? Do you know what would really honor them?
- How do you now find out what honors others? Do you keep a journal? Notes in a contact manager or daily planner?
- What have you done recently to personalize an act of recognition, whether a thank-you note or a big gift?
- How many cultures are represented among your workforce? Are you aware of how each of these cultures expresses appreciation and responds to recognition?
- What have you recently done to "culturalize" recognition?
- How much time do you typically spend in thinking about what would make an act of recognition special and unique for the person? Is it enough?

CHAPTER EIGHT

The Fifth Essential
Tell the Story

In the new world of business, where it's every executive's job to make sense of a fast-changing environment, storytelling is the ultimate leadership tool.
>   —ELIZABETH WEIL, writer[1]

cott Adams, creator of the extraordinarily popular *Dilbert,* tells the following story about his own beginnings as a cartoonist.[2]

You don't have to be a "person of influence" to be influential. In fact, the most influential people in my life are probably not even aware of the things they've taught me.

When I was trying to become a syndicated cartoonist, I sent my portfolio to one cartoon editor after another—and received one rejection after another. One editor even called to suggest that I take art classes. Then Sarah Gillespie, an editor at United Media and one of the real experts in the field, called to offer me a contract. At first, I didn't believe her. I asked if I'd have to change my style, get a partner—or learn how to draw. But she believed that I was already good enough to be a nationally syndicated cartoonist.

Her confidence in me completely changed my frame of reference: it altered how I thought about my own abilities. This may sound bizarre, but from the minute I got off the phone with her, I could draw better. You can see a marked improvement in the quality of the cartoons I drew after that conversation.

Adams's story illustrates what we described earlier in talking about the second essential (expect the best): the positive impact of our belief in another's abilities. His story also illustrates another critical element in encouraging the heart. It shows us the power of storytelling as a means of persuasion. Adams's case makes the principle come to life; it makes it authentic.

THE STORY IS THE REALITY

The world of business—the world Adams satirizes so well—loves to talk in numbers. We're inundated with financial statements, income statements, balance sheets, and stock tables. Numbers are so prevalent that we have come to accept them as real. But numbers are abstractions from reality; the *story* is the reality.

To Adams's readers, there's more truth in four panels of cartoon figures than in most of what they get from their own companies. Want evidence? Compared to the number of *Dilbert* cartoons, how many company memos and reports do you see posted in cubicles? This is because, just as in his true tale of Sarah Gillespie, Adams tells a story of some "truth" in people's working lives. It's a reality that people have experienced or observed. In fact, Adams says many of his ideas come from his readers. No matter that there is in the material world no Dogbert, or Dilbert, or pointy-haired boss in the company. Even though Adams's view reflects a cynical side of organizational life, it's a life that many have known, seen, felt, or can relate to.

Storytelling is how we pass along lessons from generation to generation, culture to culture. The past is a parable; the future is a fable. Storytelling is *the* most basic form of communication—more prevalent and more powerful than facts and figures. People also believe stories more than they believe numbers.

"Oh, come on," you say. "You've got to be kidding! You mean to say that stories are more believable than hard statistical data?" Yes, that seems to be the case. First we offer the data, which seems a bit ironic given our last point, but let's take a look.

Stanford University organizational sociologists Joanne Martin and Melanie Powers studied the impact of stories on MBA students, an often numbers-driven, highly competitive, skeptical audience. Martin and Powers compared the persuasiveness of four methods of convincing the students that a particular company truly practiced a policy of avoiding layoffs.[3] In one situation, Martin and Powers used only a story to persuade people. In the second, they presented statistical data that showed that the company had significantly less involuntary turnover than its competitors. In the third, they used the statistics and the story. In the fourth, they used a straightforward policy statement made by an executive of the company.

Which method do you think was most believable to the MBA students: (1) story only, (2) statistics only, (3) statistics and story, or (4) policy statement? The answer is, as you've probably anticipated, the story only. The students in the groups that were given *only* the story believed the claim about the policy more than any of the other groups and remembered it better several months later. You might also have suspected that the executive delivering the policy statement was the least convincing.

The renowned trial attorney Gerry Spence—who, by the way, has never lost a criminal trial—says that "the strongest structure for any argument is *story*." He goes on to illustrate his point:

Storytelling has been the principal means by which we have taught one another from the beginning of time. The campfire. The tribal members gathered around, the little children peeping from behind the adults, their eyes as wide as dollars, listening, listening. The old man—can you hear his crackly voice, telling his stories of days gone by? Something is learned from the story—the way to surround and kill a saber-toothed tiger, the hunt for the king of the mastodons in a far-off valley, how the old man survived the storm. There are stories of love, of the discovery of special magic potions, of the evil of the warring neighboring tribes—all learning of man has been handed down for eons in the form of stories.[4]

Isn't Spence's story-about-stories a wonderful example of the point that he's making? It puts the message in a context and makes it come alive. "Yes," we say at the end. "Yes, that *is* how we learn."[5]

STORIES TEACH, MOBILIZE, AND MOTIVATE

We're inundated with bits and bytes of information every nanosecond of every day. How can we possibly sort through it all and remember even a morsel? Research clearly demonstrates that information is more quickly and accurately remembered when it is first presented in the form of an example or story.[6] Researchers have found, for instance, that when American history textbooks were translated into the story-based style of *Time* and *Newsweek*, students were able to recall up to three times more information than they were after reading a more typical school text.[7]

University of Michigan business professor Karl E. Weick has studied how we make sense of the often complex and contradictory decisions and events that go on daily in our organizations. What is necessary in sense making? Says Weick, "The answer is, something that preserves plausibility and coherence, something that is reasonable and memorable, something that embodies past experience and expectations, something that resonates with other people, something that can be constructed retrospectively but also can be used prospectively, something that captures both feeling and thought, something that allows for embellishment to fit current oddities, something that is fun to construct. In short, what is necessary in sense making is a good story."[8]

Since 1985, scientist and researcher Gary Klein has been studying and writing about how people make decisions under conditions of extreme emergencies. He's taken a look at professionals in high-stakes, intense-time-pressure environments where a decision could mean life or death—people like firefighters, critical care nurses, paramedics, pilots, nuclear plant operators, and battle planners. One of Klein's conclusions flies in the face of what is almost an accepted truth in the business community. He's discovered that under emergency situations, the classic model of decision making in which people generate opinions and make deliberate choices is *not* how they function. Instead they use a nonlinear approach that involves intuition, mental simulation, metaphors, analogies, stories, and other less rational means—better known to most of us as "gut feelings." In discussing his research, Klein says, "The method we found most powerful for eliciting knowledge is to use stories."[9] He believes that storytelling is an essential skill for passing along the lessons that we learn from highly complex, challenging situations.

Patrick Kelly, founder of Physician Sales and Service (PSS), a $1.3 billion company with nearly four thousand employees, puts it this way: "We've never had a policy manual. The way we pass along our values is to sit around the campfire and share stories."[10] To pass along those values to the rest of the world, he's put it all in a book, *Faster Company*, in which he reports: "Now I have something to put in the hands of all my employees and say, 'This is the way we treat each other. This is the way we treat our customers. If you understand this, you'll make it here, and we'll all be extraordinarily successful. *This is our story.'*"[11]

Like PSS, 3M has always been a storytelling culture. One of the most often-told business stories in recent memory, in fact, is how a 3M scientist was looking for a way to replace the bookmarks in his church hymnal and eventually ended up developing the Post-it Note. 3M is now capitalizing on their storytelling tradition to rewrite the book on strategic planning.

Gordon Shaw, 3M's executive director of planning and international, became uncomfortable, it seems, with how "3M's business plans failed to reflect deep thought or to inspire commitment. They were usually just lists of 'good things to do' that made 3M functionally stronger but failed to explain the logic or rationale of winning in the marketplace."[12] He searched for a fresh approach and came up with "strategic narratives." As Shaw, along with professors Robert Brown and Philip Bromiley (from the University of Minnesota), wrote about this approach, "Planning by narrative is a lot like traditional storytelling. . . . When people can locate themselves in the story, their sense of commitment and involvement is enhanced. By conveying a powerful impression of the process of winning, narrative plans can motivate and mobilize entire organizations."[13]

Isn't that the point, after all—to motivate and mobilize? Stories are better able to accomplish these objectives than are bulleted points on an overhead. Well-told stories reach inside us and pull us along. They give us the actual experience of being there and of learning what is really important about the experience.

Because storytelling has been found to be so crucial to learning, sense making, decision making, motivating, and mobilizing, it's no wonder that we and other leadership researchers have stressed how effective storytelling is as a leadership tool. For example, Howard Gardner, the Harvard professor of education who has done extensive research on the development of human intelligence, argues that "the artful creation and articulation of stories constitutes a fundamental part of the leader's vocation. Stories speak to both parts of the human mind—its reason and emotion. And I suggest, further, that it is *stories of identity*— narratives that help individuals think about and feel who they are, where they come from, and where they are headed—that constitute the single most powerful weapon in the leader's literary arsenal."[14]

Building on the work of Gardner, University of Michigan leadership scholar Noel Tichy says of his own leadership studies, "This brings me to what I believe is the ultimate hallmark of world-class champion leaders, which is the ability to weave all the other elements together into vibrant stories that lead their organizations into the future."[15]

As Tichy points out, stories are crucial to leading organizations into the future. They are equally important in encouraging people to continue the quest toward an elusive future, especially in times of great challenge and turmoil. The climb to the top is arduous and steep, and we need encouragement to continue the ascent. Stories are essential means of conveying that we are making progress and that the actions people are taking are enabling us to get there.

Stories put a human face on success. They tell us that someone just like us can make it happen. They create organizational role models that everyone can relate to. They put the behavior in a real context and make standards more than statistics. Stories make standards come alive. They move us and touch us. By telling a story in detail, leaders illustrate what everyone needs to do to live by the organizational standards. They communicate the specific and proper actions that need to be taken to resolve tough choices. They bring people together around the campfire to learn and have fun.

It's interesting to note that the word *story* is short for the word *history*. They both have the same root and fundamentally mean the same thing. A story is narrative on an event or series of events, just like history. Coincidentally, as we pointed out earlier, the word *recognition* means "knowing again." In a very real sense, recognition *is* a story. It's something we can recall and retell whenever we need to know again who we are, what we stand for, and where we are going. That's why it's so essential that we tell the story when we recognize someone for doing the right thing or doing things right.

HOW TO TELL A GREAT STORY

According to researcher Klein, a good story is a blend of several ingredients. Here are the ones he sees in the stories he collects:

- Agents: the people who figure in the story
- Predicament: the problem the agents are trying to solve
- Intentions: what the agents plan to do
- Actions: what the agents do to achieve their intentions
- Objects: the tools the agents use
- Causality: the effects (both intended and unintended) of carrying out the actions

- Context: the many details surrounding the agents and actions
- Surprises: the unexpected things that happen in the story[16]

Let's apply Klein's framework to a recognition story and see how applicable it is. To do this, let's go back to the story that began our discussion of the seven essentials of encouraging the heart, the one Tom Melohn told about Kelly. (If you wish to refresh your memory, you could go back and read it again in its entirety in Chapter Two.)

- Is there an agent in Melohn's story? Yes, Kelly.
- Predicament? Kelly is faced with the problem of figuring out what to do with two components that won't fit together. He's also faced with the prospect of rejecting a part in a "no-reject" culture. If he throws away the part, he is not living up to the NATD standards. From Melohn's telling of the story, you can almost get inside Kelly's head. You can imagine Kelly saying to himself, "If I throw these components out, then it will mean that they'll be scrap. That violates our standard of 'no rejects.' What can I do so that I don't waste them?"
- Intentions? It's clear from the rest of the story that Kelly intended to get the rod and cylinder to fit together and to make sure he lived up to the standard of no rejects. Kelly told Melohn (and Melohn told the NATD employees) that he had come up with the inventive idea of putting the metal rod in the freezer to see if it would shrink.
- Actions? Kelly tried out his idea. He put the rod in the freezer.
- Objects? A freezer and two metal components, a rod and a cylinder.
- Causality? "It worked." The effect of the action was that the rod and cylinder fit together, and the no-rejects standard was maintained.

- Context? The recognition took place in the setting in which the incident occurred: right there on the plant floor. Melohn even managed through his reenactment to bring the actual freezer into the story. Not only did Melohn tell the story, he reenacted it. It was more than a story; it was almost a play.
- Surprises? Putting the metal rod in the freezer was an unexpected action. Additionally, Melohn's reenactment during the ceremony itself was full of surprises.

Try constructing a story like this the next time you are about to engage in an act of recognition. Here are some practical guidelines:

1. **Identify the actors.** Make sure that you clearly have in mind a person you are trying to recognize. If it's more than one person, as when a team of people is involved, name every one of them. Don't just say "the folks in accounting" or "the national account managers." Name names.
2. **State the predicament.** Present both the problem to be solved *and* the standard that is at stake. Don't pass up the chance to remind people of the values and principles involved here. It's one thing to praise people for solving a problem, but it's more powerful to also praise them for living up to the organization's beliefs.
3. **Clarify the actor's intentions**. In your recognition story, relate what went through the person's mind as he weighed his options. To do this, of course, you're going to have to talk to him about the incident. This goes back to the essential of paying attention. You can't tell a good story if you don't pay attention.
4. **Describe the actions.** Relate in as much detail as you can what happened. What did the person do, specifically? If

you can, reenact the process. It's important to describe the behaviors because the next time others are faced with a similar predicament they can recall "what Kelly did." They have a model of the kind of action they ought to take. The actions that they do take may not be precisely those that someone else did, but at least they have a framework for action.

5. **Include the props.** Like props in a play, objects are important to a story. They give it detail, and they help people put themselves into the predicament. Objects may be inanimate, or animate (as with people). There may be a protagonist and an antagonist. There may be natural elements involved. This is your opportunity to add richness to the story, to make it come alive with detail.

6. **Tell how it ended.** Don't leave them hanging; tell them the punch line. Tell the listeners what happened in the end and why it was important.

7. **Paint—or reenact—the scene.** Be sure to place all of this in context. Relate where and when it happened. Talk about the surrounding circumstances. Set the stage; paint the scene. Again, if you can actually take people to the place where it occurred, all the better.

8. **Include a surprise.** Every great story includes some kind of surprise. If at all possible, find a way to add an element of amazement. It adds interest, makes the story more memorable, and produces more fun. It might even get a laugh.

Recognition stories that include all these elements require time and preparation. Good storytelling is an art, and like any art it requires practice. But if you accept that storytelling is as effective a leadership tool as we've learned it is, then the practice and preparation are well worth the investment.

A FEW WORDS ABOUT TECHNOLOGY

Storytelling is best experienced live and in person. It's the only way we can truly sense the emotion of the storyteller and the audience. Body language, tone of voice, excitement, anticipation: the intensity of stories comes when we are there. We listen to recorded sessions of our favorite musicians because we can't always attend a live concert; so too with enjoying books instead of live readings by our favorite authors and watching videos of seminars by our favorite teachers. One of the wonders of technology is that it can capture the music, lyrics, images, and expressions for us to experience vicariously. We can listen, watch, learn, and enjoy again and again.

So too can stories about our colleagues' triumphs at work be communicated with the magic of technology. On our own voice-mail system at work, for example, every week we hear several examples of what a colleague did that was above and beyond the call of duty. The beauty of this is that not only leaders leave the messages; the technology is available for everyone to use.

So don't forget voice mail and e-mail. Don't forget the Websites, the company newsletters, and even the water coolers. Low-tech or high-tech cultures of caring and support are built story by story, and we're fortunate in our times to have available numerous media for the telling.

REFLECTING ON
TELLING THE STORY

- When was the last time you told a public story about someone who did something extraordinary in your organization?
- How effective a storyteller would you say you are?

- How comfortable are you at telling stories in public? What, if anything, is getting in your way?
- To what extent is storytelling a tradition in your organization? In your family?
- Who's the best storyteller you know personally? How can you find ways to learn from this person?
- When you make presentations, do you tend to rely more on the bulleted-point style or the narrative style? Why?
- When was the last time you were effective at telling a story that motivated and mobilized people? Recall the story, and write it down. From your point of view, what made it effective?
- What are the stories that are told most often in your organization? What are the lessons, the morals, that are being communicated? Are these the lessons that should be communicated? What other stories should be told?
- Using Klein's list of ingredients of a story, analyze one frequently told story in your organization. How well does it meet the criteria? How can it (and others) be improved to be more effective in retelling?
- When was the last time you broadcast a voice-mail or e-mail message to the entire organization telling them a story about someone who did something right or did the right thing?
- When was the last time you wrote a recognition story for your organization's newsletter? If you don't have a newsletter, how about just circulating a memo?

CHAPTER NINE

The Sixth Essential
Celebrate Together

Celebrations infuse life with passion and purpose. They summon the human spirit.
—TERRENCE E. DEAL and M. K. KEY, *Corporate Celebrations*

A uthor Hal Zina Bennett tells an uplifting story, set in his parents' small furniture factory, that illustrates the power of public recognition and celebration. During the Christmas rush, his father always hired extra workers, and since they were temporary hires motivation was often a problem. One day, Bennett's dad installed what he called a "bragging board" at the entrance where employees hung up their coats. Whenever he wanted to acknowledge an employee for an achievement, he wrote a quick thank-you note and pinned it to the bragging board for all to see.

People appreciated the notes, of course, and they left them pinned to the board in public view rather than taking them down and storing them in a private place. Then they started attaching their own notes to the board, announcing achievements and even family events outside of work that they wanted to brag about. Pretty soon notes such as "I'm a grandma! First one!" began to appear on the board, usually with a photo of the new baby. One proud parent even pinned up a perfect report card that her son brought home from school. The bragging board helped create a sense of community and camaraderie. It said this factory was a place where your humanness mattered. The bragging board story also demonstrates that people love to *participate* in celebrating achievements and special milestones in their lives.

All individual recognitions in some way can be made group celebrations. When we think of celebrations, we often imagine very elaborate events. Though celebrations are often magnificent affairs, they can be very simple too. We want to broaden the definition of celebration to include the small as well as the grandiose. The critical ingredient is togetherness. The Bragging Board served that purpose, turning a thank-you for one person into a community affair.

A CULTURE OF CELEBRATION

Terrence Deal and M. K. Key argue in their book *Corporate Celebration: Play, Purpose, and Profit at Work* that "celebration is an integral element of culture, and . . . provides the symbolic adhesive that welds a community together. But there's more than that. Without transition ritual and ceremony, businesses cannot adjust to changing circumstances. In many different ways, celebration serves as an organization's heart. This is an alternative to the view that an organization's brain—information, analysis, and strategy—is the core."[1] Scholarly research offers further support for the contention that celebration influences performance. In one study, for example, the investigators found that what distinguished high-performing groups from those performing less well was the wide variety and frequency of celebratory events—events where recognition and appreciation were expressed.[2]

The folks at The MathWorks demonstrate how true this is. The MathWorks is definitely characterized by a culture of celebration. Founded in 1984, today it's a privately held 450-person software company based in Natick, Massachusetts. If you hang out there for a while, you'll find enough examples of ritual and ceremony to fill an entire book.

The tone is set with their weeklong orientation for new employees. There are the usual things that we all cover in our orientation programs, but then The MathWorks adds a few unique twists. At the end of an exhausting week including such activities as packing the product, listening in on sales and customer service calls, and spending an hour in president Jack Little's office talking, new hires then play a Jeopardy-like game about the company.

Celebrating accomplishments has become part of the culture at The MathWorks. Take, for instance, their tenth anniversary. They wanted to mark the milestone differently, so they designed an amazingly elaborate scavenger hunt. Organizers even stealthily reprogrammed the voice-mail system for that one day so that it could be used to get clues. All over the headquarters building, cross-functional teams searched for hidden treasures. For two hours, employees scampered about cheerfully as they playfully relived the history of the company.

When MATLAB 5, an upgrade of their software product, was released, the company constructed a nine-hole miniature golf course on two floors of the building. When the company had its first $5 million month, Little called a company meeting and asked everyone to reach under their chairs. There they found hundred-dollar bills taped to the bottom. Then there are the summer outings. Every summer, employees and their families enjoy a weekend of golf, hang gliding, mountain biking, parties, and the like. The whole thing is organized by Little and his wife, Nancy.

On a smaller scale, there are the "Dove Bar" celebrations. Whenever a group completes a new product, Little sends out an e-mail message and invites everyone to join him at 2:00 P.M. around an ice cream cooler parked right outside the project leader's door. Employees get to enjoy a taste treat, while the project team members receive congratulations from their colleagues. At least once a quarter at The MathWorks, some group puts on a skit for the company; when we spoke to them last, it was the finance department's turn.

The company once wanted to say thanks to the system services and office services groups for their tireless dedication during a stressful growth period, so people planned a surprise event with home-baked goods. Because systems services and office services are always doing things for others, this gesture of thanks to them was, as one member put it, "one of the most encouraging things we've done."

In sales they have the Tas Award—a stuffed Tasmanian Devil doll—that is given to someone who goes above and beyond. There's a Technical Support Award involving a five-to-ten-minute celebration, and there are WOW! boards in the operating and technical support area for posting e-mails, letters of appreciation, and so on. The imaging processing team sends out WOW! e-mails. There's the "Poke It with a Stick Award," the "Oyster Award," and the "Water Purifier Award." There are outings to the theater and tours of Boston; The MathWorks folks may even take in a movie in the middle of the day.

The MathWorks also believes it has a social mission: to contribute to the community of which it is a part. So many employees at The MathWorks participate in a major social auction once a year.

How did The MathWorks become this kind of workplace? According to Lori Lester, manager of employee relations and training, "It goes back to The MathWorks's fundamental belief that we serve our people first." She adds, "It keeps me here. It keeps me coming back." Apparently, it keeps a lot of people coming back.

To some, The MathWorks culture of celebration might seem like a wasteful distraction. You can hear the Scrooges saying, "We haven't got time for fun and games. This is a fast-paced industry, and we can't stop production for things like that. After all, this is a business." Well, there is probably no faster-paced business than software, and The MathWorks is definitely a moneymaking enterprise. What Jack Little, Lori Lester, and the others at The MathWorks know is that promoting a culture of celebration fuels a sense of unity and mission that is essential for retaining and motivating today's employees.

Yet it is so much more than that.

WE WANT TO INVOLVE OTHERS IN OUR LIVES

Our need for affiliation is what motivates us to celebrate. We want other people to share in our lives, and we want to share in theirs. People need people; otherwise we'd all be hermits. Here's a little experiment you can try to find out how true this is.

Take a tour of your facility as soon as you can. You've done it before, we know, but this time take a tour with the explicit purpose of noticing what people have sitting on their desks, stuck to their bulletin boards, or hung on the walls. Who or what are in those picture frames? A loved one, a family pet, a special friend? What awards or diplomas are visible? What paintings and posters do you see? What trophies or tributes are sitting out? What do they celebrate? What do they signify? Take the time to engage the owners in conversation about what you see.

Have you ever asked yourself why people put all these things on public display? Have you ever asked yourself why *you* put things on public display? Okay, sure, we do it for ourselves. We like to remind ourselves of what we've accomplished, of places we've been, of people we love. We like to recall the positive memories. We want to experience again the emotions of joy, wonder, love, inspiration, importance, success. We want to *feel* something. Even—or especially—at work.

We also put our mementos on display because we want to involve others in our lives. The photos, posters, and plaques are all ways of inviting people to join us in our experience. They say, "Here's something important to me. Here's something that gives me joy and meaning. Ask me about it." If we didn't want others to share in these experiences, we'd keep them hidden and secret. What is public is meant to be shared.

Remember that zebra poster we told you about in our introduction to this book? The poster is not hanging on the wall of the office just because it's pretty. It's also there to share a message that we've carried with us for years and years. We love to tell the story of the zebra to anyone who asks—and to many who don't! We want to engage people in a conversation about what is meaningful and important to us, and the poster is a way of opening up conversation. If we keep it private, we miss an opportunity for dialogue, for teaching, for fun.

What if, when you take the tour, you find no photos, no mementos, no remembrances? What if the organization frowns on such personal displays? What if the culture of your company discourages people from getting close to each other? If this is true, you should be very concerned, as a leader and as a human being, because what is at stake is not just work; it's your health and that of others.

We said it at the beginning of this book, and we'll say it again. The best leaders want to get closer to others, want to be more intimate with others, than do the poorer performers. Recent research is also telling us that not only are these leaders more likely to be successful, they're also much more likely to be healthy. Equally important, these leaders are more likely to promote the well-being of others.

Dean Ornish, M.D., is a clinical professor of medicine and world-renowned researcher in coronary heart disease. In 1998, he was featured on the cover of *Time* and other newsmagazines for his groundbreaking work on the healing power of intimacy.[3] In his book *Love and Survival,* among other things Ornish reviews a number of scientific studies that examine the impact of love and intimacy on a person's health and well-being. From his analysis, he concludes: "When you feel loved, nurtured, cared for, supported, and intimate, you are much more likely to be happier and healthier. You have a much lower risk of getting sick and, if you do, a much greater chance of surviving."[4] In fact, if you do not have anyone you feel close to, no one who'd take care of you, no one you could turn to in time of need, "you may have *three to five times* higher risk of premature death and disease from all causes"[5] (emphasis in original).

What Ornish refers to as love, others refer to as social support. Studies on social isolation, social support, and intimacy have been conducted across the United States and around the world. They've been done involving old, middle-aged, and young men and women. If you're interested—or if you're skeptical—we encourage you to review the evidence for yourself. It'll make you smile, and it'll make you weep. It also makes you stop and think about the quality of your own relationships.

The Sixth Essential: Celebrate Together

All the evidence points in the same direction. Again, here's Ornish: "When I reviewed the scientific literature, I was amazed to find what a powerful difference love and relationships make on the incidence of disease and premature death from virtually *all* causes. It may be hard to believe that something as simple as talking with friends, feeling close to your parents, sharing feelings openly, or making yourself vulnerable to others in order to enhance intimacy can make such a powerful difference in your health and well-being, but study after study indicates that they often do."[6]

It turns out that the quality of our relationships has a protective effect. The more cohesive, supportive, and loving our relationships, the healthier our immune system is and the more resistant we are to disease. Also, although it does help to have several close social relationships, even one is significantly better than none. You can have the best job in the world and make more money than Bill Gates, but if you lack close social ties you may not live to enjoy it.

As leaders, we have now learned there is something very valuable to give when we bring people together for social support: the gift of a healthier life. Based on the evidence, it is not going too far to say that leaders who make effective use of social support activities not only promote higher levels of performance but also contribute to reducing death and disease. Now, think about what that means to the organization's bottom line: celebrations are quite literally life-giving forces.

CELEBRATIONS BUILD COMMUNITY

Celebrations—whether to recognize the accomplishment of one person or to cheer the achievements of many—are opportunities to promote individual health, but also opportunities for leaders to build healthier groups. Highly visible public recognition builds the self-esteem of the recipients, and it builds a sense of community and belonging, of working together to achieve shared goals and shared victories. Deal and Key express it this way: "Celebrations infuse life with passion and purpose. . . . They bond people together and connect us to shared values and myths. Ceremonies and rituals create community, fusing individual souls with the corporate spirit. When everything is going well, ritual occasions allow us to revel in our glory. When times are tough, ceremonies draw us together, kindling hope and faith that better times lie ahead."[7]

As members of your organization interact on more than just a professional level, they're likely to come to know and care about one another. When you have a high level of participation not just in the work itself but in the celebration of achievements, you reinforce people's common stake in reaching their goals. Making people feel included is a central function of any celebration, and the more people you can encourage through well-designed and participatory celebrations, the more your organization's people grow close. We all want to feel that we are part of the team, but it's even more important to feel part of something larger than ourselves.

Celebrations, as well as participation in developing celebrations, increase the sense of belonging, of esprit de corps. In particular, participatory celebrations bring people together so that information can be exchanged, relationships can be nourished, and a sense of shared destiny can be sustained. By making achievements public, you encourage the person being recognized and the hearts of those who witness the award. You build a culture in which people feel that their efforts are appreciated and even applauded. People who count themselves as members of this community can find meaning and purpose here.

Besides, knowing that we have alternatives, who really *wants* to work for a place that has no ritual or ceremony—a boring place that celebrates nothing? David Campbell, senior fellow with the Center for Creative Leadership, says it so well: "A leader who ignores or impedes organizational ceremonies and considers them as frivolous or 'not cost-effective' is ignoring the rhythms of history and our collective conditioning. [Ceremonies] are the punctuation marks that make sense of the passage of time; without them, there are no beginnings and endings. Life becomes an endless series of Wednesdays."[8]

So, if you're tired of an endless series of Wednesdays, take time out to celebrate something. Organization development consultant Cathy DeForest provides these examples of reasons for ceremonies and rituals:[9]

- *Organizational change and transition:* expansions, reorganizations, closings, mergers, the end of an old technology and the introduction of a new one, moves to new locations
- *Success:* financial success, promotions, awards, expansions to new markets
- *Loss:* of old procedures, financial opportunities, contracts, a job, status, a colleague who has just died, an experiment that ended in failure
- *People:* team successes, founders, winners of sales contests, employee awards, individual birthdays, marriages, reunions, doing good deeds for others
- *Events:* a company's anniversary, opening day, holidays, articulation of an organization's vision
- *The unknown:* paradox, ambiguity in the marketplace

From this list, we're sure you can find something to call people together to celebrate during the next week.

Whatever you decide to celebrate and for whatever reason, do so knowing that as a leader you are bringing more joy into people's lives, and fulfilling one of the most important functions of a leader. You are strengthening a sense of community, a team spirit that will infuse your organization with greater positive energy to face the challenges of today and tomorrow.

CELEBRATIONS REINFORCE VALUES

Celebrations serve another important function. They offer opportunities to reinforce organizational values. Whether it's in honor of individual, group, or organizational achievement, celebrations communicate what's important around here. They broadcast for all to see and hear the principles that are important enough that time and money should be spent to recognize them.

Celebrations—public statements by their very nature—give expression to and reinforce commitment to key values. They visibly demonstrate that the organization is serious about adhering to its principles. So it's important to be clear about the statements you're making. What are you reinforcing? What are you saying is significant about this moment? Parties are fine, but celebrations are more than parties. They're ceremonies and rituals that create meaning. When planning a celebration, every leader should ask, "What meaning am I trying to create?" Public ceremonies crystallize personal commitments, binding people together and letting them know they're not alone.

When individuals or teams are singled out for recognition in a public event, they are held up as role models. Research shows that peers make better role models than those who are socially distant from us. Even if the president of a company were to behave consistently with our values, his would be an insufficient example. We need to see the behavior from people like us.

Public recognition offers leaders the chance to convey the message, "Here's someone just like you. You can do this!" By awarding recognition in public to a person who represents the group, you not only give her much appreciated thanks but you also provide her colleagues with an example they can emulate. They also see that one of their own is recognized for doing the right things and doing things right. They see that efforts to go the extra mile really are appreciated. They are much more encouraged to see a peer receive public praise than to see a famous person getting an award for exactly the same behavior. We may revel in the chance to watch the stars come out on Oscar night, but the genuine significance of the ceremony is most felt by the people in the theater audience. It is, after all, their peers who voted and their peers who are getting the awards.

TAKE CARE OF YOURSELF: NURTURE YOUR NETWORK

Earlier we commented on the healing power of social support. This applies as much to you, the leader, as it does to your constituents. With times as challenging as they are, it's absolutely essential to have a strong support network. You may be the bastion of courage and hope for others during challenging times, but you don't work in a vacuum. You need support as much as the people you work with do.

Trying to get support from the group you support can, at times, be like pulling yourself up by the bootstraps. Particularly during stressful times, you need to be able to turn to your own friends outside work, as well as to peers within the world of work. You need people to support you regarding specific issues. If the world is closing in around you, and you don't have good support, there's no way you're going to survive the pressure or distress you feel from the people around you. You can safely bet that the pressure and distress will be mirrored back to you in one form or another.

When the pressure is on, your personal support system can provide you not only with a place to let off steam but also with a forum for brainstorming solutions. Don't neglect or take for granted the supportive relationships in your life. If you do, the support those people can offer at a critical time may not be available to you. Pay particular attention to personal relationships in times of change or crisis. Whenever you feel the demands of striving for extraordinary accomplishment, you especially need these relationships to assist you. Whether it's in coping with excessive stress or reaching deeper into your own inner resources, friends and supporters are the medicine you need.

What does your support network look like right now? To find out, in the center of a piece of paper draw a circle about the size of a half-dollar. Write your name in it. Draw smaller circles around the big one to represent people you can turn to for personal support; draw some of them nearer to the center and some farther away.

Now think about the closest relationships you have—the people in whom you can really confide. Jot down their names in the circles nearest your name. Work quickly, writing in names as they pop into your mind. Include people to whom you've given strong social support all through your life, but don't forget people whose friendships are new in your life. Next, in the circles farther out from the center name people you can lean on, but not necessarily ones in whom you can confide your troubles.

After filling in all the names that come to mind, take a moment to study what you've done. Who can you count on? Does the sketch include people from all areas of your life? Does it include your manager or team leader? If so, where are they located in relation to you? Where have you placed your friends, colleagues, and mentors? Are there people you haven't seen for a long time and with whom you are out of touch? Think about clubs, associations, political groups, church groups, or athletic groups you belong to now or have belonged to in the past. Ask yourself how much support you feel from each of them. Determine which relationships need to be strengthened or renewed, and get in touch with those people.

If you're building an organization that encourages the heart in the ways we've discussed, the support you give others comes back to you. One sure sign that what you're doing is working is when you see that encouraging the heart is becoming everyone's responsibility. In many ways, what goes around comes around; leaders get back what they give. That's why setting an example is so important. We turn to this issue in the next chapter.

REFLECTING ON
CELEBRATING TOGETHER

- What was the most recent celebration that you held in your organization? How long ago was it? Was it too long ago?
- How frequently do you celebrate accomplishments? Is that often enough?
- How much socializing is going on in your organization? Do people have enough opportunity to get to know each other? To build networks of support?
- What are you doing to encourage networking and social support?

- How often do you take time to talk with people about the photos on their desks or the images on their walls and what they mean to them?
- When you celebrate, are you clear about the values that you are cheering?
- How are you cheering the values while also cheering the people?
- How have you used celebration to create role models for others?
- How many work colleagues, friends, and family can you talk with frankly? How many can you share your feelings with and confide in? Are there enough people for you to feel supported? Are they the right people?
- How much fun are your celebrations? Are they too routine, not enough surprises and prizes?
- Do people in your organization feel that celebrations are a waste of time or that they're too busy to stop working? What can you do about these feelings?

CHAPTER TEN

The Seventh Essential
Set the Example

We lead by being human. We do not lead by being corporate, professional or institutional.
> —Paul G. Hawken, founder, Smith and Hawken[1]

When Cary Turner took over the stores division of Pier 1 Imports, he personally called or wrote all the store managers in the company to introduce himself and thank them for their hard work. Now that he's been there for a while, according to those who work with him, he still says thank-you all the time and sends personal handwritten thank-you notes. Small gestures, perhaps, but this is how cultures of celebration and recognition are built. One thank-you note at a time. One positive role model at a time.

Turner's also prone to the outrageous sometimes. He will accept almost any challenge to inspire and encourage associates. For instance, in December 1997, when the stores as a whole achieved a 10 percent comparative store gain, he walked barefoot on hot coals. The slogan: "We're so hot, we're cool. We're so cool, we're hot." In 1996, he made a bet with his regional managers: he'd visit all of them dressed in a chicken suit if they'd significantly increase sales. They did, and he did. When a Washington, D.C., store hit $2 million in sales, and because the store manager asked him to, Turner arrived dressed as a bride to promote its bridal business. When the Northwest region increased its December sales by 11.1 percent and challenged him to do something outrageous, he parasailed over the Puget Sound and Seattle waterfront.

But it doesn't always take the outrageous to make a positive impact. Turner is well known for slapping "high-fives" wherever he goes, in the stores, in the corporate office elevator, and even with customers. It's his way of saying, "Thank you for everything you do." It's this enthusiastic connection that makes him approachable to the people who look to him for encouragement and inspiration.

A number of organizations, like Pier 1, have a reputation for being fun places to work—for being cultures of celebration and recognition. They're magnetic, attracting and retaining employees and customers far better than their competitors. People form a strong bond with these institutions and are proud to be affiliated. They enjoy being a part of the experience.

How do these organizations earn such a reputation? The most consistent answer we hear is, "Our leaders model it." Bill Miller, corporate director of employee development and senior vice president of the Moneystore, put it this way: "From the heart emanates from the top."

Over and over again, it's the same story. Wherever you find a strong culture built around strong values—whether they are about superior quality, innovation, customer service, distinctiveness in design, respect for others, or just plain fun—you also find endless examples of leaders who personally live the values. Yes, it may emanate from the top, but a culture is sustained over time because *everyone becomes a leader*; everyone sets the example.

One of the oldest observations about human behavior is that we tend to mirror those around us. If we're around someone who's sad, we pick it up. Even entering a room feeling full of vim and vigor, we find that our energy starts to leak out if we're in the presence of negative emotions. Now, think about this on a group or organizational scale. Imagine spending your days with dozens or hundreds of down-in-the-mouth people. What a depressing thought. It's enough to make anybody want to escape as quickly as possible.

But what happens to you when you enter a room full of upbeat, supportive, appreciative, and enthusiastic people? You tend to be uplifted yourself, don't you? Human beings much prefer to be around positive people than around negative ones. It's also true that leaders in the organization set the tone. Cultures of celebration thrive over time only if the organizational leaders set an example that communicates the message that "around here we say thanks, show appreciation, and have fun."

CREDIBILITY IS THE FOUNDATION

We keep relearning the lesson that it all starts with credibility. In our continuing research on the qualities that people look for and admire in their leaders, time and time again we find that, more than anything, people want leaders who are credible.[2] Credibility is the foundation of leadership. Period.

Above all, people want to believe in their leaders. They want to believe that the leaders' word can be trusted, that they do what they say. Our findings are so consistent over such a long period of time that we've come to refer to this as the first law of leadership: if you don't believe in the messenger, you won't believe the message.

Leadership credibility makes a huge difference in our performance and our commitment to an organization. We took a look at the attitudes and performance of people led by individuals who scored high on personal credibility and those led by individuals who scored low.[3] Here's what we found. When people perceive their immediate managers or their senior managers to have high credibility, they're significantly more likely to:

- Be proud to tell others they're part of the organization
- Feel a strong sense of team spirit
- See their own personal values as consistent with those of the organization
- Feel attached and committed to the organization
- Have a sense of ownership for the organization

However, when people perceive their immediate managers to have low credibility, they're significantly more likely to:

- Produce only if they're watched carefully
- Be motivated primarily by money
- Say good things about the organization publicly but criticize it privately
- Consider looking for another job if the organization experiences problems
- Feel unsupported and unappreciated

Credibility makes a difference. Among other things, loyalty, commitment, energy, and productivity depend upon it.

So, what exactly is credibility? What is it *behaviorally*? How do you know it when you see it in action? We asked these questions, and here are some of the things people told us in response:

- "Credible leaders practice what they preach."
- "They walk the talk."
- "Their actions are consistent with their words."

- "They put their money where their mouth is."
- "They keep their promises."
- The most frequent response: "They do what they say they will do."[4]

When it comes to deciding whether a leader is believable, people first listen to the words and then watch the actions. They listen to the talk, and watch the walk; then they measure the congruence. A judgment of credible is handed down if the two are consonant. If people don't see consistency, they conclude that the leader is at best not really serious about the words, and at worst is an outright hypocrite.

Constituents are moved by deeds. Actions are the evidence of a leader's credibility. This observation leads to a straightforward prescription for leader modeling:

DWYSYWD: Do what you say you will do

DWYSYWD has two essential elements: the first is *say* and the second is *do*. To set an example, leaders must be clear about their values; they must know what they stand for. That's the *say* part. Remember that our first essential to encouraging the heart is to set clear standards. We start there, because we know that's where credibility begins. But words are not enough. Leaders must put what they say into practice; they must act on their beliefs and *do*.

In the domain of leadership, however, DWYSYWD is necessary but insufficient. Doing what you say you will do may well make you credible personally, but it may not make you a credible *leader*. Leaders represent groups of people, and those constituents have needs and interests, values and visions. To set an example—and to earn and strengthen leadership credibility—those of us who want to be leaders must base our actions on a *collective* set of aims and aspirations. We must "DWWSWWD": Do what *we* say *we* will do.

DWWSWWD reveals to us the essentials leaders have to master to set an example and sustain leader credibility. We call it the "say-we-do" process, and it means that leaders must be able to:

- Clarify their own, and others', values and beliefs
- Unify constituents around shared values
- Intensify their commitment to shared values by living the values daily and constantly reinforcing others' behavioral commitment

If you want to create and sustain a culture of celebration and recognition, you've got to set the example. Your actions send signals about who you are and about what you expect of others. If your constituents are able to see and hear you thanking people for their contributions, telling stories about their accomplishments, and taking part in celebrating successes, then chances are that you see them doing the same.

At one company we studied, the folks in management development wanted to make sure that leaders in the organization recognized the power of modeling. So they founded the "Signal Corps." Its singular mission was to promote the importance of *example* and *signals.* Their Signal Corps Creed pointed out how important each encounter with employees was in impressing upon them the appropriate behaviors. Each encounter was seen as a moment of truth during which leaders could leave either a good or a bad impression. Signal Corps members pledged to be constantly mindful of creating a good impression—one consistent with organizational values. Their behavior, they knew, spoke louder than their words.

All leaders need to heed this creed. When it comes to sending a message throughout the organization, nothing communicates more clearly than what the leaders *do*.

Lt. Gen. Daniel W. Christman knows a lot about leader modeling. He's the superintendent, or "the Supe," of West Point, the U.S. Military Academy, and a former assistant to the chairman of the joint chiefs of staff. It's his job to know how leaders set the example. In 1997, at a bonfire rally before the Army-Navy football game, in thirty-degree weather, Christman ripped open his army shirt to reveal a huge *A* painted on his chest. Needless to say, the cadets went crazy at the sight of the Supe cheering on their team.[5]

Painting your chest may not be your thing. Walking on hot coals may not be your thing either. That's not the point. The point is that directly and visibly showing others that you're there to cheer them along sends a positive signal. You're more likely to see others do it if you do it. It's that simple.

You also have more credibility if you ask others to encourage the heart. They're more likely to believe you're serious about it. To excel as a leader, you must come to terms with the fact that people believe what you do, not what you say.

START YOUR MORNING WITH ENCOURAGEMENT

We can't think of a better way to start the day than to offer someone encouragement. Why not set a positive tone bright and early by expressing how much you appreciate the contributions of others?

John Schallau, a sales engineer at Centigram Communications Corporation, thinks he should do so. Schallau created a reminder notice that pops open every day when he turns on his computer first thing in the morning. He simply lists some of the ways he might say thank you, and he occasionally adds to the list as he discovers new ways to encourage the heart. Here's a sampling of what's on Schallau's computer screen:

Rewards for Individuals
   Tickets to events
   Weekend getaway
   Attendance at industry event
   Dinner or evening on the town
   Spa visit, or weekend retreat
   Attendance at outside seminar
   Magazine subscriptions
Acknowledging Group Milestones
   Afternoon at the beach
   Park picnic
   Miniature golf
   Baseball game
   Office party with award presentations
   Lunch or dinner with staff and spouses at nice restaurant
Token Items for Giveaway Rewards
   T-shirts with company logo
   Gym bags
   Coffee mugs
   Beer or wine glasses
   Pen-and-pencil sets
Theme Days to Encourage Camaraderie
   Hawaiian Shirt Day
   Ugly Tie Day
   Sweater Day
   Costumes on Halloween Day

Food (to Recognize Events)
  Donuts
  Bagels
  Special lunch meetings
  Pizza
  Catered breaks

We love Schallau's computer reminder notice. It illustrates the most basic of all principles of how people change their behavior: change happens only when you take a first step, and then it progresses one step at a time. Schallau decided he needed to do more to recognize individual contributions and celebrate team accomplishments, so he made himself a list so that everyday there'd be something on it he could do.

Author Anne Lamott tells a wonderful story about making progress toward our goals. Although her story is about writing, we think the lesson is applicable to leadership:

> Thirty years ago my older brother, who was ten years old at the time, was trying to get a report on birds written that he'd had three months to write, which was due the next day. We were out at our family cabin in Bolinas, and he was at the kitchen table close to tears, surrounded by binder paper and pencils and unopened books on birds, immobilized by the hugeness of the task ahead. Then my father sat down beside him, put his arm around my brother's shoulder, and said, "Bird by bird, buddy. Just take it bird by bird."[6]

The possibilities for encouraging the heart seem endless. Author and educator Bob Nelson proves that in his books *1,001 Ways to Reward Employees* and *1,001 Ways to Energize Employees.*[7] All you have to do is get started. Just pick one of Nelson's 2,002 ways—or one of our 150 ways in Chapter Twelve. Schallau did that with his recognition reminder. Here are a couple more examples of how some other folks took on the challenge of improving their efforts to encourage the heart.

LEADERS GO FIRST

Sonya Lopes is school reform coordinator at the Turnbull Learning Academy, a public elementary school in San Mateo, California. She also manages the organization development and change process in the school. As she puts it, "I'm an advisor-critic-listener-reflective partner-confidante to the principal." Inspired by the book *301 Ways to Have Fun at Work,* by Dave Hemsath and Leslie Yerkes,[8] Lopes decided that she didn't want any more opportunities for fun to pass her by. So she started by displaying the word *Fun!* in a few key places. She put it on a sign by her office door so she could see it whenever she walked out. She put it in her daily planner as a bookmark. "It helped me," she said, "become more proactive in the search for 'fun' opportunities." For example, one week she had people turn in their "regular old staff meeting questionnaire" by making the completed survey into paper airplanes and flying them to her. Lopes reported that "for the first time ever, *everyone* turned in his or her questionnaire!"

Lopes started talking to everyone about having fun at work. While grocery shopping one day, she bought a box of apple cinnamon muffin mix expressly to make them for staff members. She made eight huge muffins, and on each one she wrote a reason for leaving muffins and tea bags in staff mailboxes. Inspired by Lopes's spirit of uplifting hearts, the PTA got involved in creating a livelier school environment during Teacher Appreciation Week. They even decorated the staff bathrooms with tables; potpourri; colorful wall hangings; and color, color, color. "Teachers," she said, "talked about it for *days.*"

Lopes reports that she received smiles, hugs, and notes for the actions she took. She also saw the environment change. Most important of all, Lopes learned a lesson that everyone who begins this journey learns. "Encouraging the heart of others encouraged *my* heart. As I was going around smiling, looking at people and saying their names, I became uplifted! I felt *excited* while making muffins and attaching notes to them as spirit lifters for teachers. And simply telling people a retreat I'm organizing will have *fun* as one of its top five priorities has led to curiosity from teachers as to what we will be doing." The mirror reflects back the image you portray.

Mary Anne Wellman, corporate counsel for Quantum Corporation, had a similar experience when she decided to "live with" encouraging the heart. Wellman took it beyond her work and incorporated encourage the heart at home, at MBA school, and even with strangers:

> If I saw someone wearing a sweater that I found particularly attractive, rather than admiring it in silence I complimented the person. Sometimes they were surprised, but more often they were pleased. When I returned from my recent trip to Alaska, I brought back the usual souvenirs for my daughter. However, this time I also took the time to pick out a few culinary items from the region (candies, paté, etc.) to set out in the break room on my first day back in the office. While leafing through a mail-order catalog, I saw a silver pin depicting three girls. The artist who designed and made the pin named it "The Three Sisters." I ordered three pins and gave one each to my two sisters, and I kept one. It had been a long time since any of us had given the other a gift "just because."

In the process of making encouraging the heart part of her lifestyle, Wellman also tried hard to listen more actively to her daughter, Katie. Wellman learned from her listening that her daughter wished for more time with her mom. So Wellman responded with weekly mom-and-daughter outings to Starbucks for coffee and hot chocolate. "A few weeks ago," Wellman told us, "Katie asked me why I thought about doing this. I told her I had been listening to her lament about not being able to spend enough time with me and that I thought this would be a nice way to let her know what a good job she was doing and how proud I was of her. Was this OK with her? She was thrilled. I am still not sure which was more encouraging for Katie: our weekly chats at Starbucks or that I heard what she was asking for."

Personal involvement is what setting the example is all about. Terri Sarhatt, customer services manager of the Applied Biosystems Division of Perkin-Elmer, learned how important this is even in situations where the rewards are tangible. Sarhatt was looking for a way to increase the amount of supportive communication she had with employees at the company, and as luck would have it, her decision to get personally involved coincided with the annual distribution of stock options. At Applied Biosystems, as in many high-tech companies, people often receive stock options when they've had a good year, and since Applied Biosystems has been growing at around 20 percent for the last few years, it's a regular occurrence.

In years past, Sarhatt would receive the options from her manager. She would then present them to her direct supervisors and request they do the same with their direct reports. In 1998, she decided to take a different tack. Wanting to thank folks directly, she asked her direct supervisors if they'd mind her meeting with each of their employees who were going to receive stock options. Her direct reports thought it was a terrific idea.

"I personally thanked them for the *specific* projects and the work they had done," said Sarhatt. "The employees were surprised that I would actually take the time out of my busy schedule to sit down with each of them separately and have a cup of coffee and discuss their accomplishments. One of my supervisors informed me later that her employee appreciated the time I spent with her more than she appreciated the actual stock options!" Just as with Wellman's daughter, it was the gift of personal time that mattered.

This brief sampling from Turner, Schallau, Lopes, Wellman, and Sarhatt demonstrates that when you encourage the heart, most of what you do *are* the little things. And that's the point. It doesn't take a grand plan to begin to set an example for encouraging the heart. It doesn't take a huge budget, it doesn't take psychotherapy, and it doesn't take the boss's permission. The most critical thing in all these examples was that the leaders took the initiative. Encouraging the heart became a priority.

Setting the example for encouraging the heart starts, in fact, by giving yourself permission to do so. It starts with putting it in your daily planner. It starts with putting a sign by your door. It starts when you talk to everyone about it. It starts when you turn a routine task into something fun. It starts by giving to others first. It starts when you get personally involved. When leaders do get personally involved in encouraging the heart, the results are always the same: the receiver and the giver both feel uplifted. The reflection in the mirror is the one you portray.

REFLECTING ON
SETTING THE EXAMPLE

- When you look in the mirror at work, what do you see? Do you see a smiling face? Do you see a serious face? A sad face? A mad face?
- How does the environment in your workplace reflect your behavior?

- Name one thing that you've done in the last week to encourage the heart at work. How about at home?
- What have you consciously done recently to send a signal to people that encouraging the heart is important to you?
- How personally involved are you in the recognition and celebrations that now go on in your organization?
- What would happen if you posted a sign outside your door that said "Let's have fun!"?
- What would happen if you made encouraging the heart part of your daily life—lived with it—as Wellman did? What is the first thing that you'd do?
- How many special ways can you demonstrate your appreciation of others in your workplace?
- Who is the most credible person in your workplace? Analyze what he or she does that brings them credibility. How can you incorporate these attributes into your habits?
- Can you add just one more thank-you into this week's schedule?

PART THREE

CHAPTER ELEVEN

Finding Your Voice

And the truth of your experience can *only* come through in your own voice.
— ANNE LAMOTT, *Bird by Bird*

S o far, you've been reading about others' experiences with encouraging the heart. We've offered you examples of leaders who exemplify each of the seven essentials, and we've provided ample evidence that encouraging the heart can produce extraordinary results. In the final chapter, we list 150 methods and techniques to boost your own efforts to do even better. But there's one more critical message to tuck away in your knapsack as you continue down your leadership path.[1]

You cannot lead out of someone else's experience. You can only lead out of your own.

In his witty book *Management of the Absurd*, psychologist and chief executive officer Richard Farson writes, "In both parenthood and management, it's not so much what we *do* as what we *are* that counts. . . . There is no question that parents can and should do worthwhile things for their children, but it's what they are that will really matter. . . . The same dynamic occurs in management and leadership. People learn—and respond to— what we are."[2]

Farson has nailed it. All the techniques and all the tools that fill the pages of all the management and leadership books—including this one—are not substitutes for who and what you are. In fact, they boomerang if thrown by some spin-meister who's mastered form but not substance.

People don't follow your technique. They follow you—your message and your embodiment of that message.

Max De Pree, former chairman and CEO of Herman Miller, the Michigan furniture maker, tells a moving story that well illustrates this point:

> Esther, my wife, and I have a granddaughter named Zoe, the Greek word for "life." She was born prematurely and weighed one pound, seven ounces, so small that my wedding ring could slide up her arm to her shoulder. The neonatalogist who first examined her told us that she had a 5 to 10 percent chance of living three days. . . .
>
> To complicate matters, Zoe's biological father had jumped ship the month before Zoe was born. Realizing this, a wise and caring nurse named Ruth gave me my instructions: "For the next several months, at least, you're the surrogate father. I want you to come to the hospital every day to visit Zoe, and when you come, I would like you to rub her body and her legs and her arms with the tip of your finger. While you're caressing her, you should tell her over and over how much you love her, because she has to be able to connect your voice to your touch."
>
> Ruth was doing exactly the right thing on Zoe's behalf (and, of course, on my behalf as well), and without realizing it she was giving me one of the best possible descriptions of the work of a leader. At the core of becoming a leader is the need always to connect one's voice to one's touch.[3]

De Pree goes on to explain for leaders "a prior task—*finding* one's voice in the first place."[4]

Finding your voice is absolutely critical to becoming an authentic leader. If you can't find your own true voice, you end up with a vocabulary that belongs to someone else, mouthing words that were written by some speech writer who's nothing like you at all.

Finding one's voice is something that every artist understands, and every artist knows that finding a voice is most definitely not a matter of technique. It's a matter of time and searching—soul searching.

Several years back, Jim and Donna Kouzes attended a retrospective of painter Richard Diebenkorn's work with an artist friend. Toward the end of the gallery walk, the friend made this observation: "There are really three periods in an artist's life. In the first, we paint exterior landscapes. In the second, we paint interior landscapes. In the third period, we paint our selves. That's when you begin to have your own unique style." This is the most important art appreciation lesson we've ever received. It applies equally to appreciation of the art of leadership.

When first learning to lead, we paint what we see outside of ourselves, the exterior landscape. We read biographies and autobiographies about famous leaders. We read trade books by experienced executives and dedicated scholars. We attend speeches given by decorated military officers. We buy tapes of motivational speakers, and we participate in training programs with skilled facilitators.

We do all this to master the fundamentals, the tools, and the techniques. We're clumsy at first, failing more than succeeding, but soon we can give a speech with ease, conduct a meeting with grace, and praise an employee with style. It's an absolutely essential period. An aspiring leader can no more skip the fundamentals than can an aspiring painter.

Finding Your Voice

Then it happens. Somewhere along the way, we notice how that last speech sounded mechanical and rote, how that last meeting was a boring routine, and how that last encounter felt terribly sad and empty. We awaken to the frightening thought that the words aren't ours, that the vocabulary is someone else's, that the technique is right out of the text but not straight from the heart.

This is a terrifying moment. Having invested so much time and energy in learning to do all the right things, we suddenly see that they're no longer serving us well. They seem hollow, and we feel like phonies. We stare into the darkness of our inner landscape, and we begin to wonder what lies inside.

For aspiring leaders, this awakening initiates a period of intense exploration. A period of mixing and testing new ingredients; of invention; of going beyond technique, beyond training, beyond copying what the masters do, and beyond taking the advice of others. And if you surrender to it, after exhausting experimentation and often painful suffering you come to the third period. From all those abstract strokes on the canvas emerges an expression of self that is truly your own.

Most leadership development is still at stage one. It's still mostly about painting exterior landscapes, mostly about copying other people's styles and trying to mimic the great leaders. We hope to encourage you to move beyond stage one and enter that dark inner territory, so that you can emerge into the light, where you find your own true voice.

IT'S ABOUT CARING

Poet David Whyte has written that "the voice throws us back on what we want for our life. It forces us to ask ourselves, Who is speaking? Who came to work today? Who is working for what? What do I really care about?"[5]

Finding your voice begins by asking yourself Whyte's questions. When you speak, who is speaking? Is it your voice, or someone else's? Who came to work today: did you show up fully, or was it only part of you that made it? Which part? What are you working for? What do you *really* care about: fame? fortune? power? family? people? achievement? freedom? happiness? security? wisdom? what?

It's important to answer these questions for yourself—to find your true voice—because in truth you can't lead others to places you don't want to go yourself. If you don't feel a burning passion for something, how in the world can you inspire and encourage others to share it? Until you get close enough to the flame to feel the heat, how can you know the source?

There's another possibility. Maybe people don't want to follow you to where you want to go. But they don't know that for sure until *you* know for sure.

The answers to these questions come only if you're willing to take a journey through your inner territory—a journey that requires opening doors that are shut, walking in dark spaces that are frightening, and touching the flame that burns. But at the end is truth.

Along this journey, there is one truth that you absolutely must confront. When we began this book, we said that at the heart of effective leadership is genuine caring for people. The truth that must be confronted is this: *How much do you really care about the people you lead?* Our hunch is that you care a lot. You probably wouldn't be reading a book entitled *Encouraging the Heart* if you didn't. But the question must be confronted daily, because when you care deeply, the techniques that we describe present themselves as genuine expressions of your caring. When you care little, they're perceived as nothing more than gimmicks, and you're thought of as a phony.

This was taught to us many years ago by then-Major Gen. John H. Stanford. He has since moved on from the army to become the superintendent of schools in the Seattle Unified School District, but his words are as significant today as they were then. We repeat this lesson almost every time we give a speech or conduct a seminar, and we offer it again here.

We asked Stanford if he'd tell us how he would go about developing leaders. He replied:

> When anyone asks me that question, I tell them I have the secret to success in life. The secret to success is to stay in love. Staying in love gives you the fire to really ignite other people, to see inside other people, to have a greater desire to get things done than other people. A person who is not in love doesn't really feel the kind of excitement that helps them to get ahead and lead others and to achieve. I don't know any other fire, any other thing in life that is more exhilarating and is more positive a feeling than love is.

At the time we talked to him, "staying in love" was not the answer we expected. But after all these years of studying the subject, we've found no better secret to becoming the best leader you can be than to stay in love. When you're in love with the people you lead, the products and services you offer, and the customers and clients you serve, you just pour your heart into it.

We know you can learn to lead. But don't confuse leadership with position and place. Don't confuse it with structures and systems, or tools and techniques. They're not what earn you the respect and commitment of your constituents. What earns you their respect in the end is whether you *are* what you say you are, and whether what you are embodies what they want to become.

So who *are* you, anyway?

CHAPTER TWELVE

150 Ways to Encourage the Heart

E ncouragement comes wrapped in packages of all kinds. We've seen it done in quiet ways with a thank-you, a story, and a smile; and we've been part of grand Academy Awards–style productions. Your imagination is the only limit.

This chapter gives some ideas to get you started. Most are collected examples of what we've observed and what others have contributed to us. Use what we list here as a way of stimulating your creativity. Adapt the ideas to your situation; combine them or use them singularly.

We've categorized the ideas under the seven essentials so you can focus your attention on those areas you most feel in need of working on. But as you see, many of these actions include elements of more than one essential.

Most important, have fun with this. These activities are designed to facilitate your learning, and learning to do a better job of encouraging the heart should be a joyous process.

1. Take time to clarify the values or "operating principles" that are important for you and your team to live by. Write down your answer to this question: "What are the values that I believe should guide my daily decisions and actions, and those of the people with whom I work and interact?" We sometimes refer to this as the "credo memo" exercise. It's like a note you send to your colleagues before you take off for an extended sabbatical, telling them that while you're not around these are the principles you want them to use to govern their actions and decisions.

2. Ask your associates—those with whom you work regularly—to do the same exercise.

3. Keep current. If you've already done the exercise in item one, get out the piece of paper on which you wrote your values and ask yourself, "To what extent do these *still* represent the values that I believe should guide our daily decisions and actions? Is there anything I want to add? Anything I want to delete? Any priorities I want to change?"

4. Post your values statement conspicuously where you know you'll be reminded of your principles regularly. Put a copy in your wallet. Put one in your planner. Put it on your bulletin board over your desk and on your computer as a yellow sticky. Martin Luther actually nailed his beliefs on the cathedral door centuries back, and it started quite a movement! Why not you?

5. Make the topic of one of your next team meetings "Our Values." Ask everyone to state aloud what they believe in. Listen and observe. What are the values that everyone seems to share in common? What values seem to be unique

to some individuals? Are there any major values conflicts? Talk about how you can honor individual values and yet as a team have common values that govern your collective behavior. Post collective values in visible places all around your workplace common areas.

6. If your organization has a corporate creed, or some kind of published statement of values, then set yours, your team's, and the organization's values credos side by side. To what extent are they compatible? To what extent are there some conflicts? How good a fit is there between organizational and personal values? What needs to be changed? What needs recommitment?

7. Every time you start a new project, make sure that SMART goals (specific, measurable, attainable, results-oriented, and time-bounded) are set. It's best if people set their own, but prescribed goals are better than no goals. Make these goals visible and accessible to everyone working on the team.

8. Make sure people get regular, specific feedback. Remember what we learned from the research: the combination of feedback plus goals is encouraging in and of itself. When people know where they're headed and how far they've gotten, they feel better, are physically healthier, and achieve higher levels of performance. So make sure that people get feedback on their progress toward goals regularly. It might come from you: "Hey, we've reached a project milestone. Well done. Let's celebrate!"

9. Better yet, create ways for people to monitor themselves so they know how much progress they've made. The software we're using to write this book enables us at any instant to compute how many pages, words, paragraphs, lines, and characters we've written. We know what our contract asks for in the number of pages, and we know

the deadlines. We're completely self-monitoring. That sure feels better than getting bugged by the editor every day, asking, "What progress are you making? How are you doing?"

10. The next time—and every time—you recognize an individual or a group for doing the right thing or doing things right, make sure to announce the standard. Announce it at the beginning, and repeat it at the end. Say something like, "One of the things we stand for around here is knock-your-socks-off service to our customers. Just yesterday, Bev did something to exemplify that value. Let me tell you about it. . . . And remember, just as Bev did, let's knock their socks off every time!"

11. If your company gives bonuses, start looking for ways to link some portion of the bonus to how people are meeting or exceeding the cherished values of the organization. When it's time to hand out the checks, attach a short note mentioning the actions that exemplified the values. At one company we've worked with, 33 percent of the bonus-eligible managers' incentive is directly linked to the extent to which they've lived out the values. Their ratings come from their direct reports. Now, that's putting your money where your mouth is.

12. Take a class or read a book on how to set goals.

13. Take a class or read a book on how to give performance feedback.

14. Participate in a retreat, the purpose of which is to explore meaning and purpose in life and work.

15. Think of someone you admire who exemplifies living a principle-centered life. Interview that person. Find out how they discovered their own values.

16. Invent or select some symbolic ways of visibly marking people's progress, as the scouts and the military do. Pins,

ribbons, badges, patches, medals, certificates, etc., that signify "You made it to the next level" send meaningful messages to the receivers and their friends, families, and colleagues.

17. Watch *Eyes on the Prize*, the film on the civil rights movement, the next time it's on TV, or rent it at the video store. It's a compelling story of the power of purpose and the dedication people make to realizing a dream.

18. Keep your eyes on the prize!

THE SECOND ESSENTIAL: EXPECT THE BEST

19. Remember the principle of the self-fulfilling prophecy: people tend to act consistently with your expectations of them. The Pygmalion effect also applies to you, so be positive and optimistic about your own ability to lead, as well as about the achievements of the people around you. How? Surround yourself with positive people who can remind you of your strengths and abilities.

20. Practice smiling. This is not a joke. Smiling and laughing release naturally occurring chemicals in our bodies that fight off depression and uplift our moods. Try it.

21. Ask yourself this question: "Do I honestly believe everyone on my team can achieve the goals we've set and live by the values we've agreed upon?" If your answer is yes, make sure that you communicate this to them verbally and nonverbally. If your answer is no, figure out what you can do to change your answer to yes. What changes have to be made, in you and in them, for that to happen? Make them. You can do it.

22. The next time you talk to one of your constituents about a difficulty she's having with a project, make sure that

sometime during the conversation you say, "I know you can do it," or words to that effect. And you better mean it.

23. Assign people to important tasks that aren't part of their defined job. Let them know you have assigned them these unusual jobs because you have strong belief in them—that you believe they have the capacity to excel at it. Make a binding commitment to supply them the training, resources, authority, and coaching they need to be successful.

24. Like Don Bennett's daughter (Chapter Five), the next time someone is struggling to succeed, find a way to walk beside him for the most difficult part of the climb, telling him, "Come on, you can do it. I know you can do it. You're the best in the world."

25. Practice envisioning. Right now, picture a sunset at the beach, the waves washing against the shore. Picture a gently flowing stream in the middle of a cool forest on a warm day. Picture a meadow of yellow wildflowers in full bloom in springtime. Picture a hundred-foot waterfall rushing to a valley floor in early spring as the snow melts. Can you imagine these scenes? Do you get a picture in your mind's eye? Of course you do. Sit down with another person and describe these scenes to each other in all their rich color and texture. The ability to create mental images and clearly communicate them to others is a critical leadership skill.

26. Apply this same visualizing ability to imagine scenes in your mind's eye of what you want to accomplish as a leader. Picture yourself and your team reaching the summit of your aspirations, whatever that might be currently. Describe the scene to others in great detail just as you described the sunset at the beach in the previous item. Get others to join you. Create a richly textured image of your future, and see it, smell it, taste it, hear it, touch it. Make

it as real as possible. The better you are at doing this, the more likely your group will reach higher levels of performance. It's no fantasy.

27. Buy a few inspirational posters and put them on the walls of your facility. If you don't like the ones in the catalogues, then find posters of images that symbolize the spirit you'd like to promote in your workplace. Through these or other means, find some way to make your positive expectations visible.

28. Walk around your facility and examine the images that are on the walls. Are they images that communicate positive messages or negative ones? Analyze your company's annual report, your own and your executive's speeches, the company newsletter, and other forms of corporate communication. Are the messages positive or negative? Do whatever you can to change the images to positive ones. Remember what historian Fred Polak said (in Chapter Five) about the rise and fall of cultures. When images are positive, cultures and organizations are in ascendance.

29. The next time you are involved in coaching or training people in acquiring new knowledge or a new skill, make sure you say out loud that you know this skill is something that can be acquired. Tell them they can learn it. Even if you think this is obvious, say it out loud anyway. It's important to send the message to your learners. Of course, you've got to believe it yourself, so if in reality you don't think a particular skill can be learned and that it's innate instead, then please do everyone a favor and don't accept an assignment to teach it.

30. It's often said that the real way to tell if someone is a leader is by how many constituents become leaders themselves. Who in your organization has this kind of reputation?

Who has a reputation for inspiring, uplifting, and developing esteem in others? Ask around if you don't know. Observe what these individuals do by asking to shadow them for a couple days. Ask them for pointers on how they do what they do well.

31. Read the children's story *The Little Engine That Could* to your child or someone else's child. Ask the child about something she thought she couldn't do but did. What was that like? What helped the turnaround? Apply your insights to your organization.

32. Read George Bernard Shaw's *Pygmalion*. This is the classic novel on the power of positive expectations. Or rent and watch the video of *My Fair Lady*. The film version of Shaw's novel, it portrays the power of belief in self. Watch how Eliza Doolittle evolves through a growing sense that she can learn.

33. Learn how to meditate. Practice it daily. Get in touch.

34. Listen to a tape on mental imagery and mental rehearsal. Practice it daily. (Caution: this is one kind of tape you don't want to listen to in your car.)

35. Visit your local library and rent a video or CD of Martin Luther King's "I Have a Dream" speech delivered at the Lincoln Memorial in Washington, D.C., in 1963. Listen to it for the word pictures he paints. You'll be able to see what he says. Now try to add word pictures to your own speeches.

THE THIRD ESSENTIAL: PAY ATTENTION

36. Leave your desk for fifteen minutes every day, solely for the purpose of learning more about each of your key constituents. Who are they? What are their needs and aspira-

tions? What do they need to find greater joy in their work? How do they like to be rewarded?

37. When you're out there caring by wandering around (CBWA), take along a pocket notebook to record the things people are doing right and the right things people are doing. Make sure to record not only the names but also the details about setting, people involved, how the act is special, and how it fits with the standards you're trying to reinforce. Use this later when telling your recognition stories.

38. Make note, also, of the kinds of "gifts" or recognition people appreciate (or don't appreciate). Remember, for some people, all that glitters is not gold!

39. Start a file of recognition ideas on your computer or in a journal that you can carry in your briefcase, purse, or pocket. Record in it ideas that come to you for recognizing and rewarding individual contributions and for celebrating team accomplishments. Keep your eyes and ears open for those moments we all encounter when we experience or witness particularly effective events of this sort. You might also pick up some ideas from television dramas, movies, or books. A journal where you can jot down these ideas becomes a tool for remembering good ideas and also for focusing your search for new ways to encourage the heart.

40. Don't wait for a ceremony as a reason to recognize someone. If you notice something that deserves immediate recognition, go up and say something like, "I was just noticing how you handled that customer complaint. The way you listened actively and responded was a real model of what we're looking for. What you've done is an example to everyone. Thank you." If you happen to be carrying around a few extra coupons for a free drink at

the local coffee or juice shop, here's an opportunity to give one out.

41. Get a small annual calendar with space to write the birthdays of your key constituents. Also write in it the anniversary dates of their joining the organization. Send a note or drop by for a visit on those dates.

42. Walk in another's shoes for a while. Volunteer to do someone's job. Roll up your shirtsleeves and jump in. People appreciate your efforts, and you gain a better understanding of what your colleagues do.

43. Wander around your workplace for the express purpose of finding someone in the act of doing something that exemplifies your organization's standards. Give that person recognition on the spot.

44. Make a short list of those people who are performing their work above stated expectations. Pay particular attention to those who best embody the team's values and priorities. Then jot down at least three ways to single out these people and praise or reward them over the next couple of weeks. Don't wait too long to put your plans into action.

45. Imagine that someone has followed you around with a video camera and filmed your daily wanderings. Now imagine that you are watching the video. What behavioral signals are you sending? Are they ones that communicate that you're looking for people doing things right and doing the right things? Or do they announce that the sheriff's in town? What specific behaviors can you adopt that communicate *I'm here to find all the positive examples I can*?

46. Make a list from memory of the objects that each of your key constituents has in her workspace. Once you've done this, go pay a visit to see how accurate your memory is. Now go spend time with the people whose workspaces you couldn't recall—in their space.

47. If you're a virtual company and don't have the opportunity to visit everyone you work with, ask people to describe to you in detail their workspace. Ask them probing questions about what's on their desk, what's on the walls, etc. Tell them you're trying to get a feel for their space in the same way that you do with the people down the hall whose space you actually do see.

48. Right now, pay attention to your breathing. What do you notice? Write it down. Your ability to attend to the most common and immediate elements of your daily life helps you be more attuned to what is going on around you.

49. Right now, pay attention to your heartbeat. What do you notice? Write it down.

50. Right now, pay attention to the sounds in your immediate space. What do you notice? Write it down.

51. Next time you go to the movies, stay for the credits. Pay attention to how the makers of the film manage to recognize virtually everyone who took part. Can you do that with everyone who works on the "movie" you're making right now? If not, invent a way to make sure that you can capture the names and contributions of everyone. Think about the end of your movie, and watch the credits roll.

52. The next time you watch an awards ceremony like the Oscars, pay particular attention to which acceptance speeches you like and which you don't like, and why. Incorporate the best of these ideas into acts of recognition that you carry out.

53. The next time you listen to someone talk about himself, his work, and what's important, listen with your "eyes and heart," not just your ears and brain. What do you notice in listening with eyes and heart that you don't in listening with ears and brain?

54. For the next lunch hour, hang out at the table with your team. At our company's Palo Alto office, Friday is pizza-for-lunch day. The company buys, and we all sit around and chat about "stuff." There's no agenda. We just get to know each other and talk about whatever's on our minds.

55. At your next team meeting, disclose something about yourself that others don't know. We're not talking deep dark secrets here, just something that enables others to get to know you a little better: the number of brothers and sisters you have, what it was like growing up in your house, your first memory of working in the organization, your favorite screw-up of all time, anything that makes you more open to others. Encourage the same in them. Remember, openness leads to trust, and trust is essential to your personal credibility. Try practicing more openness.

56. Ask your colleagues for feedback about your performance, particularly about how you are doing in encouraging the heart. The ground rules are that you can only ask questions for clarification and that you can only respond by saying thank you.

THE FOURTH ESSENTIAL: PERSONALIZE RECOGNITION

57. Think back on a time when someone encouraged your heart meaningfully and memorably. What did she do to make it special for you? How did she personalize it for you? Make note of the lessons you learned, and apply them.

58. Tell people in your organization your own "most meaningful recognition story." Ask them to tell theirs. What are the common lessons?

59. Talk with friends outside of work. Ask them to tell you stories about receiving recognition that particularly moved or affected them. Sometimes, great ideas can come out of such talks because you can share the inner experience of how people are affected by having their efforts acknowledged.

60. The next time you give a speech on behalf of your organization and you have to wear a name tag, wear the name of someone in your organization other than yours. (Maj. Gen. John Stanford did that once when he gave a speech at Santa Clara University. He wanted to communicate how important his aide-de-camp was to him, so he wore that person's name tag.) Notice how it feels to do this. How might it feel to be the other person, knowing that you're wearing his name tag?

61. At the end of one of your speeches, say something like, "My colleagues at Challenge, Inc., couldn't be with me today. I sure hope I represented them well."

62. As they now do at many airlines, give your customers, vendors, and other employees coupons to award to people who do something exceptional. Make it possible for these coupons to be redeemed for some kind of prize.

63. Make every effort to personalize every recognition event so that the man or woman receiving it feels uniquely appreciated. For the avid bicyclist in your office, for instance, recognize them with a small plastic model of a bike for the desktop; attach a note that says, "For a quick spin around the block when you're working late."

64. Try doing what Carl English did (in Chapter Seven): write a thank-you note to a loved one of the person in your organization who has done something special.

65. Send champagne or sparkling cider and flowers to the family of your next Super Person of the Month.

66. Invite the recipient's family to attend a special-recognition ceremony.

67. Every time you plan an act of recognition, ask yourself, "What can I do to make sure this is special, dramatic, and unique for this person? How can I do the equivalent of putting a motorized flag on the machine, or a part in the freezer, or a letter addressed to the associate's son?"

68. Every time you plan a recognition ceremony and expect to present some kind of gift, ask yourself, "Is this something the individual would appreciate?"

69. Create symbols for certain kinds of recognition in your organization. We use the zebra. It's just amazing how many zebra T-shirts, zebra cups, zebra mugs, zebra pencils, zebra pins, zebra cards, and zebra what-have-you there are! Be creative devising your rewards; have some fun with them.

70. Enlist the help of someone who knows well the person you intend to recognize. Ask him what the person likes, what would make it special. Through this sort of grassroots involvement, you are more likely to personalize while linking rewards to actual performance.

71. Publish captioned photos or the names of people you want to recognize in a company newsletter, annual report, or department handout. If there's room, include a brief story describing the person's special contribution.

72. Create your organization's Hall of Fame: an area for small plaques, or even handwritten notes, recognizing all the people who've done extraordinary things.

73. Your imagination and creativity are the only limits to personalizing recognition. Use them both.

74. Make a contribution to an employee's favorite charity and announce it at a company party or department get-together.

75. Display banners in the company cafeteria, with the name of the person or persons being thanked.
76. Take a class or workshop on creativity.
77. Take a course in drawing, painting, or photography.
78. Learn to use a software program for creating exciting graphics.
79. Take a course about advertising and promotion to study words and images that inspire people; translate those methods into encouraging the heart.
80. Say thank you personally every time you appreciate something someone does, anywhere and anytime. It's good practice, and good manners.
81. Make a vow that never again will you fail to personalize every recognition you make, every celebration you hold.

THE FIFTH ESSENTIAL: TELL THE STORY

82. More than likely, you are planning to recognize some individual or group in the next few days. Whatever else you do, be sure to tell the story of what was done in as much detail as you can. If possible, figure out a way to reenact the incident. There must be someone in your organization who is a great storyteller; spend some time talking with her about how she came to be so good at it. Pick up whatever tips you can.
83. At the next opportunity, tell someone the story of your most meaningful recognition.
84. Make the only agenda item for one of your team meetings that each person tells the story of his or her most meaningful recognition.
85. Make the only agenda item of another team meeting the telling of stories on the theme of "I heard something good about you," related to someone they work with.

86. Never pass up any opportunity to publicly relate true stories about how people in your organization have gone above and beyond the call of duty. Hallways, elevators, cafeterias, as well as meeting rooms are all acceptable venues for telling a good story.

87. If at all possible, whenever you give out recognition try to do it in the place where the accomplishment actually occurred. If that's not feasible, at least make sure to describe the scene to people so that they can picture it in their own minds. All good stories create a sense of place.

88. Don't forget voice mail and e-mail; these are good media for telling stories as well. Although people tend to want shorter stories in these formats, they're still helpful ways to disseminate good news.

89. Keep a journal. Record in as much detail as you can the critical incidents of the day. Capture as many examples of outstanding and commendable performance as you can. The practice of observing and recording is important in building your skills in storytelling.

90. Take a page out of 3M's book, and incorporate storytelling into your next strategic planning process. Pledge that you will no longer accept bulleted points on overheads as an acceptable plan for the future.

91. What's the best movie you ever saw that really tells a compelling story? Rent it on video and watch it again. What lessons can you learn from your favorite movie? How can you incorporate these lessons into your leadership practice?

92. Ask a professional storyteller—yes, they exist—to participate in one of your leadership seminars, and get everyone to learn some tips on good storytelling.

93. Buy a CD or tape of one of your favorite children's stories. Listen to how a professional tells a story. Try reading the story yourself in the same way the professional does.

94. At the next holiday when you're together with your family or friends, volunteer to read a story fit for the occasion.
95. Take a class in storytelling. Attend the next storytellers' convention in your town.
96. At dinner every night, don't just talk about the day; tell a story about it. Describe the rich details of place, people, and feelings. Use your home as a practice stage.
97. Attend a reading at a local bookstore featuring a fiction writer you like. Listen to how he reads his stories. Learn from his example how to express yourself in stories.
98. Take an improvisational-theater class.
99. Interview an actor who does improvisational theater. Ask her to share some ways of taking a simple idea from the audience and turning it into a story.

THE SIXTH ESSENTIAL: CELEBRATE TOGETHER

100. Every celebration has a potential dual purpose. One is to offer social support, something that we know makes people happier, healthier, and higher-performing. The other is to honor an individual, group, or entire organization for upholding a cherished standard. While we celebrate Independence Day with fireworks, food, drink, and fun, we also celebrate the value of freedom and those who have dedicated their lives to keeping us free. Organizational celebrations have this same function. Make sure to ask yourself about the fundamental principles that are being honored as well as how we're going to have fun.
101. Visit a party store in your neighborhood. You can pick up countless ideas on how to make something more festive.
102. Visit an organization that you know has a reputation for being a really fun place to work (The MathWorks and

Southwest Airlines are just two examples). Find out what makes them so inventive when it comes to celebration.

103. Attend local athletic events. Watch cheerleaders, coaches, and players as they celebrate small and large victories. Focus on their enthusiasm and energy. Watch how people express this enthusiasm as well as how those who receive it are affected. Notice how *you* are affected by the celebrations.

104. At a wedding or other celebratory event, make mental notes on what you like, or what really inspires you about the event. See if you can incorporate some of these ideas into your plans for encouraging the heart.

105. If your organization doesn't do much celebrating, start an informal celebration task force. It probably has to be a skunk-works operation, since, with a few notable exceptions, CEOs don't tend to sponsor these kinds of projects. Make it your job to liven up the place, borrowing where you can from the inventiveness of others and creating your own fun and games at work.

106. Put up a "bragging board" in your workspace. Post notes of appreciation from customers, vendors, and colleagues. Invite everyone to contribute notes and pictures of themselves and others.

107. End each of your team meetings with a round of public praising.

108. In times of change and transition, people need to get together to talk about how they're feeling and doing. Social support is most critical at times like this so schedule regular opportunities for people to lean on each other. It might even be helpful for you to get an outside facilitator to work with your group if the situation is particularly intense.

109. Be sure to mark particularly significant transitions with special celebrations—things like company anniversaries,

a merger or acquisition, the launch of a new product, etc. You might not be able to build a temporary nine-hole miniature golf course in your building (as The MathWorks, in Chapter Nine, did), but what else can you do to make the event unique and memorable?

110. Give every celebration a theme, and always include a surprise at some time during the evening.

111. Formal events are important, but informal ones are likely to be more frequent and accessible. Organize informal ways to bring people together: special lunches, picnics, noontime athletic events (volleyball, shooting baskets, softball game, etc.), anything that promotes camaraderie and interpersonal support.

112. When organizing a celebration, make sure everyone knows what it's about: dates, reason for celebration, where it is to be held, how people become eligible to take part. We all know how it feels to be left out, so pay particular attention to communicating these occasions.

113. Get people involved in planning celebrations. But don't try to do it all yourself. Joint planning offers social support, gets people to laugh together, and generates more creativity than if one person handles everything.

114. Show up in a costume at your next group celebration. Hey, if Sam Walton, at one time the richest man in America, was willing to put on a hula skirt and dance on Wall Street, then we all have permission to dress in a clown suit for a special event. Besides, people love it when they can laugh with the boss like that. Herb Kelleher of Southwest Airlines and Harry Quadracci of Quad Graphics (to name a couple of CEOs) have made big successes out of their public displays of playfulness.

115. Put a microwave in the vicinity of your office door. At about 3:00 P.M. each day, cook up some popcorn. Invite

folks to take a break and join you for a brief discussion about how the day's going. If popcorn isn't your thing, how about an ice cream vending machine or a basket of fruit?

116. Always keep a few party favors handy. You never know when you might want to throw a spontaneous celebration should an employee announce a wedding, a birth, or other personal achievement.

117. Always keep a few spare tickets to the local cinema in your drawer. Surprise someone with a night out for two (or more) at the movies.

118. Just for the heck of it, around noon someday soon, say to everyone, "Let's go to the movies," and go take in a matinee.

119. Print up note cards that say at the top, "I heard something good about you. . . ." Leave enough blank space for people to write a personalized note to a coworker, describing the particular situation that is deemed to deserve recognition. Use them yourself to recognize your employees, but also give every employee a stack of these cards to hand out and encourage their use for recognizing one another. Provide a bulletin board in a highly visible place, where people who've received cards can display them.

120. One Southern California hospital has instituted the use of "Catch Me" buttons. Every time a manager or fellow employee notices someone doing something right, she tells him about it and presents him with her own button. The buttons are redeemed at the end of the month for prizes and awards.

121. There's a nursing home in Tennessee, adjacent to the main hospital, which recognizes its staff with a simple pin that says, "Caught caring!" In an environment where patients often can't say thank you, these pins mean a great deal to

staff members. They represent tangible evidence that someone recognizes how much they give.

122. Plan festive celebrations for even the smaller milestones that your team reaches. Don't wait until the whole project is completed before you celebrate. Immediate acknowledgment keeps energy and enthusiasm high.

123. Set aside one day each year as a special organization-wide celebration day, much like Independence Day or Mardi Gras.

124. Go to clown school so that you can learn to laugh and joke around more. Humor is something people look for in leaders. And that's no joke. (Ouch!)

125. Once a quarter, go out for an evening at the local comedy club. Some of them offer classes. Take some lessons if you can.

126. At one of your next meetings, make the only agenda item discussion of how people are feeling at that moment about working in the organization.

127. Take care of your own needs for support. Develop a relationship with at least one person with whom you can talk about your grandest hopes and worst fears, your greatest achievements and your biggest flops.

THE SEVENTH ESSENTIAL: SET THE EXAMPLE

128. Do a DWYSYWD audit (recall Chapter Ten). Take a sheet of paper and draw a line down the middle. On the left-hand side record your values: the principles by which you say you want to lead your organization. On the right-hand side, record your actions: what you do regularly to live out each of your values. The only way to get any value out of this exercise, of course, is to be completely

self-honest. If you don't see yourself doing anything to live out a value, then leave the space blank. If you think your behaviors are contrary to your espoused values, then write down that admission. Grade yourself on how you're doing. Do your values and actions line up? Where are you strong? Where do you have opportunities for improvement? Make a plan to better align values and actions.

129. Now do a DWWSWWD audit (recall Chapter Ten). Using the same process that you used in #128 above, assess how you are doing in living up to the values you share as a group.

130. Become more visible. You're supposed to be setting the example, and people have to see you doing what you say.

131. Get personally involved in as many recognition events and celebrations as possible. If you don't attend staff celebrations, you're sending the message that you're not interested. That lack of interest is sure to be mirrored back to you.

132. Identify those experiences in your life that truly inspire you, and then bring this kind of inspiration into your conversations with employees.

133. Write and deliver at least three thank-you notes every day. We've never heard anyone complain about being thanked too much, but we've all heard lots of complaints about being thanked too little!

134. Look around for a person you know or have heard about who is much better at encouraging the heart than you are. Ask for his advice and some coaching.

135. Ask a colleague to give you feedback on how you are encouraging the heart. Ask her for suggestions on how to improve.

136. Fit some form of caring by walking around (CBWA; Chapters Two and Six) into your daily routine. Take time

to find out what at least two people are doing to exemplify the standards that have been set. Let them know you're curious.

137. Every time you start a meeting, make sure to affirm your personal commitment to the values that you all share. There's something about frequent repetition of a commitment that starts you moving in that direction. The more people you tell and the more often you say it, the harder it is to back out.

138. Post your values where you and others can see them.

139. Ensure that you identify a positive role model for each of the seven essentials of encouraging the heart. Make sure you can envision in your mind someone who does each of these practices well.

140. Practice the seven essentials regularly and extensively. If possible, sessions should be done with a coach or trusted colleague present so that you can get feedback on how you're doing.

141. Give yourself some credit for practicing and applying the seven essentials. Find a way to reward yourself for doing what you say.

142. Like John Schallau (in Chapter Ten), create your own recognition reminder notice, screen saver, or other device for making visible the ways in which you can encourage the heart.

143. Put a sign on your door or cubicle that reads "Fun!"

144. Think of one person in your department or organization who exemplifies one of your organization's standards. Think of another person who exemplifies another standard. Find a way to make these individuals peer coaches for others.

145. Make sure that others know about your own efforts to model encouragement. Tell people stories about how you

tried and succeeded, or tried and failed. Share the lessons you've learned.

146. Keep a journal of your experiments with encouraging the heart. What works for you? What doesn't? What lessons have you learned? How has this effort changed you as a leader?

147. The next time someone recognizes you, make note of your own thoughts and feelings. (Experience becomes the best teacher, but only if we reflect on it.) Then send that person a thank-you note expressing appreciation for what you learned.

148. Offer to teach a course on encouraging the heart. The best way to learn something is to teach it to someone else. You certainly remember how much more you prepared for something when you actually had to be the one in front of the classroom.

149. Practice "living with encouraging the heart." That is, create a plan to make it part of your life, say, for a week, in which you must include some element of encouraging the heart at work, at home, in the neighborhood, while shopping, while eating out, and while participating in an athletic activity. For one week, see what it's like to live with this practice.

150. Read *1,001 Ways to Reward Employees, 1,001 Ways to Energize Employees,* and *301 Ways to Have Fun at Work* for 2,303 more ways to encourage the heart. (See the endnotes for Chapter Ten for reference information.)

Oh, and here's one more for you!

151. Now, give yourself a standing ovation for having read this book! Your desire to encourage the heart is worth celebrating. Thank you.

Get together with friends and colleagues and try to generate your own list of 150 ways to encourage the heart. Send us any of your ideas, and we'll find a way to share them with others. You can fax them to Jim Kouzes at (650) 326-7065 or Barry Posner at (408) 554-4553. Or send e-mail (jkouzes@tpgls.com or bposner@scu.edu).

Introduction

1. For a detailed description of the Five Practices of Exemplary Leadership® and the research behind them, see Kouzes, J., and Posner, B., *The Leadership Challenge* (San Francisco: Jossey-Bass, 2002). Encouraging the Heart is one of the Five Practices that we have developed and is our proprietary name for this practice.

2. *The Leadership Practices Inventory (LPI)* was developed to assess the frequency with which people engage in the Five Practices of Exemplary Leadership. Each year, more than 40,000 individual leaders complete the self version of the *LPI* and over 150,000 complete the *LPI-Observer*. We continue to find that the more frequently leaders engage in the five practices, the more effective they are as leaders on numerous measures of satisfaction and productivity. Our own database, which includes more than 100,000 respondents, validates this fact, as do more than 175 independent research projects conducted by doctoral students and academic scholars (see www.leadershipchallenge.com for more information about these studies).

Chapter One

1. See Kouzes and Posner (1995).
2. Kepner-Tregoe, *People and Their Jobs: What's Real, What's Rhetoric?* Princeton, N.J.: Kepner-Tregoe, 1995, p. 5.
3. Kepner-Tregoe (1995), pp. 7, 9.
4. Kepner-Tregoe (1995), p. 7.
5. Unless otherwise indicated, quotes and stories from individuals

in this book are from interviews conducted or case studies collected by us.

6. Kepner-Tregoe (1995), p. 7.
7. Telephone interview with Jodi Taylor, vice president, Center for Creative Leadership, Colorado Springs, Colo., Apr. 1998.
8. For a complete list of all the tools available contact, Jodi Taylor at CCL: phone (719) 633-3891, fax (719) 633-2236.
9. The FIRO-B was developed by Will Schutz. It measured two dimensions of three factors: the extent to which a person both *expresses* and *wants* (1) inclusion, (2) control, and (3) affection. See Schutz, W. *The Interpersonal Underworld (FIRO)*. Palo Alto, Calif.: Science and Behavior Books, 1966. See also Schutz, W. *The Human Element: Productivity, Self-Esteem, and the Bottom Line*. San Francisco: Jossey-Bass, 1994.
10. Goleman, D. *Emotional Intelligence: Why It Can Matter More Than IQ*. New York: Bantam Books, 1995, p. 80.
11. Quoted in Farnham, A. "Are You Smart Enough to Keep Your Job?" *Fortune*, Jan. 15, 1996, p. 36.
12. Federman, in remarks to the Leavey School of Business, Santa Clara University, Apr. 2, 1983.
13. Whyte, D. *The Heart Aroused: Poetry and the Preservation of the Soul in Corporate America*. New York: Currency-Doubleday, 1994, p. 178.
14. Fulghum, R. *All I Really Need to Know I Learned in Kindergarten: Uncommon Thoughts on Common Things*. New York: Random House, 1989.
15. Survey by Robert Half International, Inc., Menlo Park, Calif., Aug. 1994.
16. Lindahl study cited by Bob Nelson in presentation at the Center for Excellence in Nonprofits (San Jose, CA) on "Motivating Employees in the Nineties," Sept. 20, 1996.
17. Graham, G. H. "Going the Extra Mile: Motivating Your Workers Doesn't Always Involve Money." *San Jose Mercury News*, Jan. 7, 1987, p. 4C.

18. Kanter, R. M., in presentation at Santa Clara University on "The Change Masters," Mar. 13, 1986.

Chapter Two

1. To learn more about the Super Person of the Month award, see Melohn, T. *The New Partnership: Profit by Bringing Out the Best in Your People, Customers, and Yourself.* Essex Junction, Vt.: Oliver Wright, 1994, pp. 127–138.
2. *In Search of Excellence: The Video.* Video Arts, Inc., and Nathan/Tyler, 1987. Length 88 minutes. Available from Video Arts, 8614 West Catalpa Ave., Chicago, IL 60656; phone (800) 553-0091.
3. Melohn (1994), p. 225.
4. Martin, J., and Powers, M. "Organizational Stories: More Vivid and Persuasive Than Quantitative Data." In B. M. Staw (ed.), *Psychological Foundations of Organizational Behavior.* (2nd ed.) Glenview, Ill.: Scott, Foresman, 1983; see pp. 161–168.
5. Melohn (1994), p. 127.

Chapter Three

1. Bennis, W. *On Becoming a Leader.* Reading, Mass.: Addison-Wesley, 1989, p. 40.
2. Kouzes, J., and Posner, B. *Leadership Practices Inventory.* (2nd ed.) San Francisco: Jossey-Bass/Pfeiffer, 1997. For information about the LPI, contact the publisher at (800) 956-7739 or www.pfeiffer.com.

Chapter Four

1. Carroll, L. *Alice's Adventures in Wonderland and Through the Looking Glass.* New York: Bantam Books, 1992, p. 124. (Originally published 1865.)
2. This section is adapted from the second edition of *The Leadership Challenge* (Kouzes and Posner, 1995), pp. 209–219.

3. See for example Posner, B. Z., and Westwood, R. I. "A Cross-Cultural Investigation of the Shared Values Relationship." *International Journal of Value-Based Management,* 1995, *11*(4), 1–10; Posner, B. Z., and Schmidt, W. H. "Values Congruence and Differences Between the Interplay of Personal and Organizational Value Systems." *Journal of Business Ethics,* 1992, *12*(2), 171–177; and Posner, B. Z., Kouzes, J. M., and Schmidt, W. H. "Shared Values Make a Difference: An Empirical Test of Corporate Culture." *Human Resource Management,* 1985, *24*(3), 293–310.

For a related study, see also Haas, J. W., Sypher, B. D., and Sypher, H. E. "Do Shared Goals Really Make a Difference?" *Management Communication Quarterly,* 1992, *6*(2), 166–179. See also Posner, B. Z., and Schmidt, W. H. "Demographic Characteristics and Shared Values." *International Journal of Value-Based Management,* 1992, *5*(1), 77–87; and Posner, B. Z. "Person-Organization Values Congruence: No Support for Individual Differences as a Moderating Influence." *Human Relations,* 1992, *45*(2), 351–361.

For data on values and health, see, for example, Chapman, J. "Collegial Support Linked to Reduction of Job Stress. *Nursing Management,* 1993, *24*(5), 52–56; Jex, S. M., and Gudanowski, D. M. "Efficacy Beliefs and Work Stress." *Journal of Organizational Behavior,* 1992, *13*(5), 509–517; Matteson, M. T. "Individual-Organizational Relationship: Implications for Preventing Job Stress and Burnout." In J. T. Quick and others (eds.), *Work Stress: Health Care Systems in the Workplace.* New York: Praeger, 1987; Matteson, M. T., and Ivancevich, J. M. *Controlling Work Stress: Effective Human Resource and Management Strategies.* San Francisco: Jossey-Bass, 1987; Schaufeli, W. B., Maslach, C., and Marek, T. (eds.). *Professional Burnout.* Washington, D.C.: Taylor and Francis, 1993; Newman, J. E., and Beehr, T. A. "Personal and Organizational Strategies for Handling Job Stress: A Review of Research and Opinion." *Personnel Psychology,* 1979, *32*(1), 1–43.

4. Posner and Schmidt (1993), pp. 171–177.
5. Bennett, H. Z., and Sparrow, S. J. *Follow Your Bliss*. Ukiah, Calif.: Tenacity Press, 1997.
6. Csikszentmihalyi, M. *Finding Flow: The Psychology of Engagement with Everyday Life*. New York: Basic Books, 1997, p. 137.
7. Csikszentmihalyi (1997), p. 23.
8. Csikszentmihalyi (1997), p. 23.
9. Bandura, A., and Cervone, D. "Self-Evaluative and Self-Efficacy Mechanisms Governing the Motivational Effects of Goal Systems." *Journal of Personality and Social Psychology*, 1983, *45*, 1017–1028.
10. Henkoff, R. "Make Your Office More Productive." *Fortune*, Feb. 25, 1991, p. 82.
11. Squires, S. "Clinging to Hope." *San Jose Mercury News*, Feb. 25, 1984, p. 12C. See also Breznitz, S. "The Effect of Hope on Coping with Stress." In M. H. Appley and R. Trumbell (eds.), *Dynamics of Stress: Physiological, Psychological, and Social Perspectives*. New York: Plenum, 1986; Seligman, M.E.P., *Learned Optimism*. New York: Knopf, 1990; Peterson, C., and Bossio, L. M. *Health and Optimism: New Research on the Relationship Between Positive Thinking and Physical Well-Being*. New York: Free Press, 1991; Khalsa, D. S. *Longevity*. New York: Warner Books, 1997, p. 8; and Miller, E. E. *Deep Healing: The Essence of Mind/Body Medicine*. Hay House, 1997, p. 199.
12. Peck, M. S. *The Road Less Traveled: A New Psychology of Love, Traditional Values, and Spiritual Growth*. New York: Touchstone, 1978.

Chapter Five

1. See for example Jones, E. C. "Interpreting Interpersonal Behavior: The Effects of Expectancies." *Science*, 1986, *234*, 41–46; Field, R.H.G., and Van Seters, D. A. "Management by Expectations (MBE): The Power of Positive Prophecy." *Journal of General*

Management, 1988, *14*(2), 1–33; Eden, D. *Pygmalion in Management: Productivity as a Self-Fulfilling Prophecy.* Lexington, Mass.: Lexington Books, 1990; and Eden, D. "Leadership and Expectations: Pygmalion Effects and Other Self-Fulfilling Prophecies in Organizations." *Leadership Quarterly,* 1992, *3*(4), 271–305.

2. For a video overview and case examples of the Pygmalion Effect, see *Productivity and the Self-Fulfilling Prophecy: The Pygmalion Effect* (2nd ed.), available from CRM Films, 2215 Faraday Ave., Carlsbad, CA 92008; phone (800) 421-0833.

3. Melohn (1994), p. 111.

4. Manzoni, J.-F., and Barsoux, J.-L. "The Set-Up-to-Fail Syndrome." *Harvard Business Review,* Mar.–Apr. 1998, pp. 101–113.

5. Manzoni and Barsoux (1998), p. 102.

6. Cooperrider, D. L. "Positive Image, Positive Action: The Affirmative Basis of Organizing." In S. Srivastva, D. L. Cooperrider, and Associates, *Appreciative Management and Leadership: The Power of Positive Thought and Action in Organizations.* San Francisco: Jossey-Bass, 1990, p. 103.

7. For a discussion of group effectiveness and positive images, see Cooperrider (1990), pp. 108 and 115. For the original study on group images, see Schwartz, R. "The Internal Dialogue: On the Asymmetry Between Positive and Negative Coping Thoughts." *Cognitive Therapy and Research,* 1986, *10,* 591–605.

8. Cooperrider (1990), p. 114.

9. Polak, F. *The Image of the Future.* New York: Elsevier, 1973, p. 19. Quoted in Cooperrider (1990), p. 111.

10. Schmidt, W. H., and Posner, B. Z. *Managerial Values and Expectations: The Silent Power in Personal and Organizational Life.* New York: American Management Association, 1982.

11. Blitzer, R. J., Petersen, C., and Rogers, L. "How to Build Self-Esteem." *Training and Development,* 1993, *47,* 58–60.

Chapter Six

1. Bracey, H., Rosenblum, J., Sanford, A., and Trueblood, R. *Managing from the Heart.* New York: Delacorte Press, 1990, p. 6.

2. For an in-depth discussion of personal credibility, see Kouzes, J. M., and Posner, B. Z. *Credibility: How Leaders Gain and Lose It, Why People Demand It.* San Francisco: Jossey-Bass, 2003.

3. See Boyer, G. "Turning Points in the Development of Male Servant-Leaders." (Ph.D. dissertation, Fielding Institute, 1997.)

4. See for example Schmidt and Posner (1982); Posner, Kouzes, and Schmidt, (1985); Schmidt, W. H., and Posner, B. Z. "Values and Expectations of Federal Service Executives." *Public Administration Review,* 1986, *46*(5), 447–454; and Posner, B. Z., and Schmidt, W. H. "Values and the American Manager: An Update Updated." *California Management Review,* 1992, *34*(3), 80–94.

5. "New Leadership for a New Century." Peter D. Hart Research Associates, August 28, 1998.

6. Fisher, R., and Brown, S. *Getting Together.* Boston: Houghton Mifflin, 1988.

7. McCall, M. W., Lombardo, M., and Morrison, A. *The Lessons of Experience.* Lexington, Mass.: Lexington Books, 1988.

8. Srivastva, S., and Barrett, F. J. "Foundations for Executive Integrity: Dialogue, Diversity, Development." In S. Srivastva and Associates (eds.), *Executive Integrity.* San Francisco: Jossey-Bass, 1988.

9. As cited in Rice, F. "Champions of Communications." *Fortune,* June 3, 1991, pp. 111ff.

10. Ross, J. A. "Does Friendship Improve Job Performance?" *Harvard Business Review,* Mar.–Apr. 1997, pp. 8–9. See also Jehn, K. A., and Shah, P. P. "Interpersonal Relationships and Task Performance: An Examination of Mediating Processes in Friendship and Acquaintance Groups." *Journal of Personality and Social Psychology,* 1997, *72*(4), 775–790.

11. Deutsch, M. "Cooperation and Trust: Some Theoretical Notes." In R. Jones (ed.), *Nebraska Symposium on Motivation.* Lincoln: University of Nebraska Press, 1962; and Zand, D. E. "Trust and Managerial Problem Solving." *Administrative Science Quarterly,* 1972, *17*(2), 229–239.

12. Jamieson, D., and O'Mara, J. *Managing Workforce 2000: Gaining the Diversity Advantage.* San Francisco: Jossey-Bass, 1991.

Chapter Eight

1. Weil, E. "Every Leader Tells a Story." *Fast Company,* June–July 1998, p. 38.
2. Adams, S. "My Greatest Lesson." *Fast Company,* June–July 1998, p. 83.
3. Martin, J., and Powers, M. "Organizational Stories: More Vivid and Persuasive than Quantitative Data." In B. M. Staw (ed.), *Psychological Foundations of Organizational Behavior.* (2nd ed.) Glenview, Ill.: Scott, Foresman, 1983.
4. Spence, G. *How to Win an Argument Every Time.* New York: St. Martin's Press, 1995, p. 113.
5. For a similar perspective, see Conger, J. A. *Winning 'Em Over: A New Model for Management in the Age of Persuasion.* New York: Simon & Schuster, 1998.
6. Wilkens, A. L. "Organizational Stories as Symbols Which Control the Organization." In L. R. Pondy and others (eds.), *Organizational Symbolism.* Greenwich, Conn.: JAI Press, 1983. See also Armstrong, D. *Managing by Storying Around: A New Method of Leadership.* New York: Doubleday Currency, 1992.
7. For more information on this study and other story research, see Shaw, G., Brown, R., and Bromiley, P. "Strategic Stories: How 3M Is Rewriting Business Planning." *Harvard Business Review* (May–June 1998), pp. 41-50.
8. Weick, K. E. *Sensemaking in Organizations.* Thousands Oaks, Calif.: Sage Publications, 1995, pp. 60–61.
9. For a complete analysis, see Klein, G. *The Sources of Power: How People Make Decisions.* Cambridge, Mass.: MIT Press, 1998.
10. Quoted in Weil (1998), p. 40.
11. Weil (1998), p. 40. See also Kelly, P. *Faster Company.* New York: Wiley, 1998.
12. See Shaw, Brown, and Bromiley (1998).
13. Shaw, Brown, and Bromiley (1998), pp. 43, 50.
14. Gardner, H. *Leading Minds.* New York: Basic Books, 1995, p. 43.
15. Tichy, N., with Cohen, E. *The Leadership Engine: How Winning*

Companies Build Leaders at Every Level. New York: HarperBusiness, 1997, p. 173.

16. Klein (1998), pp. 177–178.

Chapter Nine

1. Deal, T., and Key, M. K. *Corporate Celebration: Play, Purpose, and Profit at Work.* San Francisco: Berrett-Koehler, 1998, p. 11.
2. Jones, M. O., and others. "Performing Well: The Impact of Rituals, Celebrations, and Networks of Support." Presented at the Western Academy of Management conference, Hollywood, Calif., Apr. 10, 1987.
3. Ornish, D. *Love and Survival: The Scientific Basis for the Healing Power of Love and Intimacy.* New York: HarperCollins, 1998. See especially pages 23–71 for a review of several significant studies on the relationship between social relationships and health.
4. Ornish (1998), p. 23.
5. Ornish (1998), p. 28.
6. Ornish (1998), p. 30.
7. Deal and Key (1998), p. 5.
8. Campbell, D. *If I'm in Charge Here, Why Is Everybody Laughing?* Greensboro, N.C.: Center for Creative Leadership, 1984, p. 64.
9. DeForest, C. "The Art of Celebration: A New Concept for Today's Leaders." In J. D. Adams (ed.), *Transforming Leadership: From Vision to Results.* Alexandria, Va.: Miles River Press, 1986, p. 223.

Chapter Ten

1. Quoted in Nelson, B. *1,001 Ways to Reward Employees.* New York: Workman Publishing, 1994.
2. For details on our research on leader credibility, see Kouzes and Posner (1995), pp. 19–31; and Kouzes and Posner (1993).
3. This relationship was first reported by O'Reilly, C. A. "Charisma as Communication: The Impact of Top Management Credibility

and Philosophy on Employee Involvement." Paper presented
to the annual meeting of the Academy of Management, Boston,
Aug. 1984.

4. Kouzes and Posner (2003), p. 47.

5. Winerip, M. "The Beauty of Beast Barracks." *New York Times Magazine*, Oct. 12, 1997, p. 47.

6. Lamott, A. *Bird by Bird: Some Instructions on Writing and Life.* New York: Pantheon, 1994, p. 19.

7. See Nelson (1994) and Nelson, B. *1001 Ways to Energize Employees.* New York: Workman Publishing, 1997.

8. Hemsath, D., and Yerkes, L. *301 Ways to Have Fun at Work.* San Francisco: Berrett-Koehler, 1997.

Chapter Eleven

1. Portions of this chapter appeared previously in *Leader to Leader* (premier issue, Drucker Foundation and Jossey-Bass, 1996, pp. 9–11).

2. Farson, R. *Management of the Absurd: Paradoxes of Leadership.* New York: Simon & Schuster, 1996, p. 34.

3. De Pree, M. *Leadership Jazz.* New York: Currency Doubleday, 1992, pp. 1–3.

4. De Pree (1992), p. 5.

5. Whyte (1994), p. 143.

When writing a book there are two things foremost in our minds—the story and the people. And you can't have one without the other. In fact, the story is the people.

In our first book, *The Leadership Challenge,* we thanked so many people one book reviewer suggested that it was like reading an additional chapter to the book, but noted that we were certainly practicing what we had preached. That's because writing is a lonely affair much of the time. We huddle for hours over a keyboard itching for something to flow out the end of our fingertips. But by the time we get to the last word on the last page, so many people have put their fingerprints on the manuscript that the list of contributors fills a chapter, and that chapter encompasses every human emotion. While writing is a solitary act—even for coauthors—we're never alone.

Encouraging the Heart is a testimony to those individuals without whom not one word would have made it to print. Our families are the first and last to share our joy and suffering. Donna Kouzes, Jackie Schmidt Posner, and Amanda Posner are always there for us. They're our inspiration, our cheering section, our sounding board, our research team, and our collective shoulders to lean on. When it comes to encouraging the heart, they exemplify what it's all about. They are our teachers. We love you so very much.

Like an invention drawn on a napkin, a book begins as rough ideas, odd-sized pieces of paper, jumbled thoughts, collections of stories, and promises to organize them all into a coherent and compelling read. That promise would not have been fulfilled if it were not for our talented colleague, Hal Bennett, who collaborated with us from the initial stages of conception. Hal is a prolific writer in his own right, and he dedicated himself to turning our original thoughts into an early draft.

Our editor, Susan Williams, kept us connected to each other and to our task. She continuously uplifted us, especially when the weight of a deadline approached. Rachel Livsey juggled this project along with about a dozen others. She's been our master coordinator, making sure we met all our deadlines and commitments. "Let's ask Rachel" was a common refrain from beginning to end, and her final comments on the closing chapter were immensely important.

Kathy Dalle-Molle is the only editorial member who has been with us for all three book projects. She secured our permissions and checked our facts and is the world's preeminent editor when it comes to attention to these details. Not a quote or a story would have made it to print without Kathy. She's a royal treasure, and we're ever so grateful for the extraordinary work she has done on all our books. And finally, the last time we saw the manuscript it was in the extremely capable hands of Mary Garrett and Judith Hibbard. Our book got produced because Mary and Judith managed the process of getting it from rough copy to bound book. To all our editorial teammates and to their supporting colleagues at Jossey-Bass, we thank you for a joyous collaboration since 1985.

Several of our colleagues at Tom Peters Group/Learning Systems guided us toward some wonderful case examples of individual recognition and group celebration, as did our MBA students at the Leavey School of Business at Santa Clara University. We owe a special thanks to Ron Crossland, Jeni Nichols, and Dick Heller for steering us toward some amazing people. And as she has often done, with great love and care Christy

Tonge reviewed our work and wrote us wonderful marginal notes—complete with stickers and stars—suggesting important additions and critical edits. Christy is our guru of authentic leadership, and she kept us true to ourselves and to the material.

There are hundreds of others who have shaped our thinking about leadership and about encouraging the heart. We thank all of those clients, colleagues, students, and friends, who have been with us on past leadership expeditions and all those who continue to share our ongoing leadership adventures. Your stories have inspired us and reminded us about the nobility of the human spirit, our capacity and empathy, and the power of love in both professional and personal relationships.

This was a fun book to write. Our thanks to all of you for encouraging our hearts over these past two decades as we've studied, practiced, taught, listened, read, observed, written, and marveled about the art of leadership.

October 1998

James M. Kouzes
Palo Alto, California

Barry Z. Posner
Santa Clara, California

Jim Kouzes is chairman emeritus of the Tom Peters Company, a professional services firm that inspires organizations to invent the new world of work using leadership training and consulting solutions. He is also an Executive Fellow at the Center for Innovation and Entrepreneurship at the Leavey School of Business, Santa Clara University.

Barry Posner is dean of the Leavey School of Business and professor of leadership at Santa Clara University (Silicon Valley, California), where he has received numerous teaching and innovation awards, including his school's and his university's highest faculty awards. Jim and Barry were named by the International Management Council as the 2001 recipients of the prestigious Wilbur M. McFeely Award. This honor puts them in the company of Ken Blanchard, Stephen Covey, Peter Drucker, Edward Deming, Francis Hesselbein, Lee Iacocca, Rosabeth Moss Kanter, Norman Vincent Peale, and Tom Peters, earlier recipients of the award.

In addition to their award-winning and best-selling book *The Leadership Challenge*, Jim and Barry have coauthored *Credibility: How Leaders Gain and Lose It, Why People Demand It* (1993)—which was chosen by *Industry Week* as one of that year's five best management books—as well as *The Leadership Challenge Planner* (1999). Jim and Barry also developed the highly acclaimed *Leadership Practices Inventory (LPI)*, a 360-degree questionnaire assessing leadership behavior; the *LPI* is one of the most widely used leadership assessment instruments in the world. More than 175 doctoral dissertations and academic research projects have been based on the *Five Practices of Exemplary Leadership*® model. CRM Learning has produced a number of leadership and management development videos based on their publications.

Jim and Barry are frequent conference speakers, and each has conducted leadership development programs for scores of organizations, including: Alcoa, Applied Materials, ARCO, AT&T, Australia Post, Bank of America, Bose, Charles Schwab, Cisco Systems, Conference Board of Canada, Consumers Energy, Dell Computer, Deloitte Touche, Egon Zehnder International, Federal Express, Gymboree, Hewlett-Packard, IBM, Johnson & Johnson, Kaiser Foundation Health Plans and Hospitals, Lawrence Livermore National Labs, Levi Strauss & Co., L. L. Bean, 3M, Merck, Mervyn's, Motorola, Network Appliance, Roche Bioscience, Siemens, Sun Microsystems, TRW, Toyota, US Postal Service, United Way, and VISA.

Jim Kouzes is featured as one of the workplace experts in George Dixon's book, *What Works at Work: Lessons from the Masters* (1988), and in *Learning Journeys: Top Management Experts Share Hard-Earned Lessons on Becoming Great Mentors and Leaders*, edited by Marshall Goldsmith, Beverly Kaye, and Ken Shelton (2000). Not only is he a highly regarded leadership scholar and an experienced executive, he's been cited by the *Wall Street Journal* as one of the twelve most requested non-university executive education providers to U.S. companies. A popular seminar and conference speaker, Jim shares his insights about the leadership practices that contribute to high performance in individuals and organizations, and he leaves his audiences inspired with practical leadership tools and tips that they can apply at work, at home, and in their communities.

Jim directed the Executive Development Center (EDC) at Santa Clara University from 1981 through 1987. Under his leadership the EDC was awarded two gold medals from the Council for the Advancement and Support of Education. He also founded the Joint Center for Human Services Development at San Jose State University, which he managed from 1972 until 1980, and prior to that was on the staff of the University of Texas School of Social Work. His career in training and development began in 1969 when, as part of the Southwest urban team, he conducted seminars for Community Action Agency staff and volunteers in the "war on poverty" effort. Jim received his B.A. degree (1967) with honors from Michigan State University in political science and a certificate (1974) from San Jose State University's School of Business for completion of the internship in organization development.

Jim's interest in leadership began while he was growing up in Washington, D.C. In 1961 he was one of a dozen Eagle Scouts selected to serve in John F. Kennedy's Honor Guard at the presidential inauguration. Inspired by Kennedy, he served as a Peace Corps volunteer from 1967 through 1969. Jim can be reached at 877-866–9691, extension 239, or via e-mail at jim@kouzesposner.com.

Barry Posner, an internationally renowned scholar and educator, is the author or coauthor of more than a hundred research and practitioner-focused articles in such publications as *Academy of Management Journal, Journal of Applied Psychology, Human Relations, Personnel Psychology, IEEE Transaction on Engineering Management, Journal of Business Ethics, California Management Review, Business Horizons,* and *Management Review.* In addition to his books with Jim Kouzes, he has coauthored several books on project management, most recently *Checkered Flag Projects: 10 Rules for Creating and Managing Projects That*

Win! Barry is on the editorial review boards for the *Journal of Management Inquiry* and *Journal of Business Ethics.*

Barry received his B.A. degree (1970) with honors from the University of California, Santa Barbara, in political science. He received his M.A. degree (1972) from The Ohio State University in public administration and his Ph.D. degree (1976) from the University of Massachusetts, Amherst, in organizational behavior and administrative theory. He's a highly regarded seminar leader and conference speaker with a warm and engaging style, full of inspiring examples and practical applications. Having consulted with a wide variety of public and private sector organizations around the globe, Barry currently sits on the boards of directors for the American Institute of Architects (AIA) and the San Jose Repertory Theater. He served previously on the boards of Public Allies, Big Brothers/Big Sisters of Santa Clara County, the Center for Excellence in Non-Profits, Sigma Phi Epsilon Fraternity, and several start-up companies. At Santa Clara University he has previously served as associate dean for graduate programs and managing partner for the Executive Development Center.

Barry's interest in leadership began as a student during the turbulent unrest on college campuses in the late 1960s, when he was participating and reflecting on the balance between energetic collective action and chaotic and frustrated anarchy. At one time, he aspired to be a Supreme Court justice, but realizing he would have to study law, he redirected his energies into understanding people, organizational systems, and the liberation of the human spirit. Barry can be reached at 408-554–4523, or via e-mail at bposner@scu.edu.

More information about Jim and Barry, and their work, can be found at their Web site: www.leadershipchallenge.com.

Expectations: aspects of, 61–72; background on, 61–64; example of, 20–21; and images, 68–69; for leadership, 69–70; methods for, 155–158; and performance, 64–67; reflecting on, 72; and self-esteem, 70–72; and storytelling, 99–100

F

Farber, S., 89–90
Farnham, A., 178
Farson, R., 145, 186
Federman, I., 11, 178
Feedback: encouragement as, 58–59; and goals, 54–58; positive, 14; soliciting, 86; and standards, 54–59
Field, R.H.G., 181
FIRO-B, 9, 10, 177–178
Fisher, R., 183
Flow, and goals, 52–53
Freer, R., 95–97
Friendship, and attention, 80, 81–82, 84–86
Fulghum, R., 12, 178

G

Gardner, H., 105, 184
Gardner, J., 33
Gillespie, S., 99
Girl Scouts, and standards, 47
Glenn Valley Homes, personalized recognition at, 95–97
Goals: and feedback, 54–58; SMART, 153; and standards, 52–54

Goleman, D., 10, 177, 178
Graham, G. H., 14, 178
Gudanowski, D., 180

H

Haas, J. W., 180
Hall, P., 45
Hanging out, and attention, 82–84
Hartwell, H., 74–75
Hawken, P. G., 129
Hay Group, 81
Hemsath, D., 138, 186
Hendricks, G., 73
Henkoff, R., 181
Higgins, H., 61–62
Honeywell-Measurex, attention at, 82–84
Houghton Winery, attention at, 77–78

I

Images, and expectations, 68–69
INSEAD, 63
Intimacy, and celebration, 119–120
Ivancevich, J. M., 180

J

Jamieson, D., 183
Japan, culture of, 94–95
Jehn, K. A., 84–85, 183
Jenkins, C., 89
Jex, S. M., 180
Johnson, K., 47, 49
Jones, E. C., 181
Jones, M. O., 185

Newman, J. E., 180
Nicolo, J., 6–7, 27
North American Tool and Die (NATD): attention at, 74; expectations at, 63; recognition at, 15–30; storytelling at, 107

O

Oak Ridge National Laboratory, and Leadership Action Consortium, 47–49
O'Mara, J., 183
Openness: and attention, 84–86; and encouragement, 6–7
Opportunities Industrialization Center West, 80
O'Reilly, C. A., 185
Ornish, D., 119–120, 185

P

Pacific Bell, recognition at, 5
Peck, M. S., 59, 181
Performance: and celebration, 114–115; and expectations, 64–67
Perkin-Elmer, example setting at, 140–141
Personalized recognition: aspects of, 89–97; background on, 89–91; and culture, 94–95; example of, 23–24; and likes, 92–93; methods for, 162–165; phrasing of, 91–92; reflecting on, 97; and thoughtfulness, 95–97
Petersen, C., 182
Peterson, C., 181

Physician Sales and Service, storytelling at, 103–104
Pier 1 Imports, example setting at, 129–130
Pin progression, for standards, 48–49
Polak, F., 68–69, 157, 182
Posner, B. Z., 51*n*, 174, 177, 179, 180, 182–183, 185
Powers, M., 101, 179, 183–184
Pritchard, M., 80, 81
Public Allies, 79
Pygmalion effect, 21, 61–64, 69, 76, 155, 158

Q

Quadracci, H., 169

R

Reality, and storytelling, 100–102
Recognition: need for, 4–5; personalized, 89–97; as reminder, 19; reminder notices for, 136–137
Rice, F., 183
Robert Half International, Inc., 178
Rogers, L., 182
Rosenblum, J., 74–75, 182
Rosenthal, R., 62
Ross, J. A., 183

S

Sanford, A., 74–75, 182
Sarhatt, T., 140–141
Say-we-do process, and credibility, 134
Schallau, J., 135–137, 141, 173

**Put The Five Practices of Exemplary Leadership®
to Work in Your Organization**

The Leadership Practices Inventory (LPI)

Over its nearly 20-year history, the LPI has become the most popular off-the-shelf 360-degree leadership assessment instrument in the world, used by nearly one million leaders worldwide. Repeated analysis of the instrument has proven it to be a reliable and valid measure of a leader's effectiveness. But most important to its creators, the results have also shown that leadership is understandable and learnable.

Leadership Practices Inventory (LPI), Second Edition, Revised

Gives managers and supervisors the skills to master the Five Practices of Exemplary Leadership: Modeling the Way, Inspiring a Shared Vision, Challenging the Process, Enabling Others to Act, and Encouraging the Heart.

LPI ONLINE

LPI Online is a time-saving, interactive tool for administering the *Leadership Practices*

Inventory (LPI). LPI Online offers simplified, time-saving administration; immediate, streamlined results; and 24/7 web-based access for LPI administrators and participants.

Leadership Practices Inventory-Individual Contributor (LPI-IC), Second Edition, Revised

This instrument is specifically designed for non-management employees, informal leaders, those involved in self-directed teams, project teams, task forces, and cross-functional teams—and helps participants evaluate their own leadership abilities.

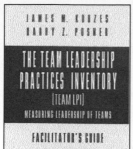

The Team Leadership Practices Inventory (Team LPI)

Ideal for all types of work teams, this instrument helps participants to identify areas for enhancing and improving leadership practices within a team setting.

Student Leadership Practices Inventory

Designed to help develop the leaders of tomorrow, it includes a self-evaluation tool and an instrument for the gathering of feedback from peers, teachers, mentors, or other individuals.

Learn Anytime, Anywhere

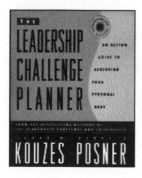

THE LEADERSHIP CHALLENGE PLANNER
An Action Guide to Achieving Your Personal Best

This stand-alone, self-directed workbook guides you through the vital steps of preparing, implementing, and evaluating your next project.

WHAT FOLLOWERS EXPECT FROM LEADERS
How to Meet People's Expectations and Build Credibility

Make better use of your commute time. These two one-hour audio cassettes provide concrete examples and specific guidance on how to become a more effective leader.

THE FIVE PRACTICES OF EXEMPLARY LEADERSHIP
When Leaders Are at Their Best

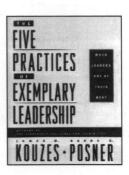

This 16-page article is perfect for leaders with limited time and budget. It provides a concise overview of Kouzes and Posner's model and overall thoughts on leadership.

LEADERSHIP CHALLENGE CARD

This handy pocket-sized card for desks, organizers, and wallets offers quick reference to the model used in *The Leadership Challenge* and the *LPI*.

Plan a Leadership Workshop

The Leadership Challenge® Workshop
This intensive two- or three-day program is based on the best-selling book and designed by its authors.

- Offered by the Tom Peters Company in onsite, public, and custom formats with pre- and post-consulting available for ongoing needs.
- Implemented by some of the world's most recognized companies, including Brooks Brothers, Cisco, Clorox, Rolls-Royce, Seagate Technology, Sun Microsystems, Unilever, and Wells Fargo Bank.

Leadership Is Everyone's Business®
A one-day workshop that develops the leadership practices of individual contributors at all levels of the organization.

To learn more about these learning opportunities, contact the Tom Peters Company in the U.S. and abroad at 888-221-8685, e-mail info@tompeters.com, or visit their website at www.tompeters.com/implementation/solutions/challenge.

Get Connected With the Convenience of Online Learning

Instigo
Working with Instigo, Jim Kouzes produced several highly interactive online seminars. They are now available to you and your organization for your next learning activity.

To learn more, visit www.instigo.com.

Create Excitement With
The Leadership Challenge Video Collection

Video programs offer a compelling format for leadership training in both small groups and large gatherings. These *Leadership Challenge* videos are designed to educate, inspire, and liberate the leader in everyone.

Leadership Challenge: This compelling video shows that leadership is attainable; it is not the private preserve of a few charismatic people but a learnable set of practices.

Leadership in Action: Based on the best-selling book *The Leadership Challenge,* this must-have video describes the five practices common to all successful leaders through a single case study.

Closing the Leadership Gap: This exceptional video reveals how to cultivate and maintain credibility and fill the leadership gap—when leaders say one thing and do another.

Encouraging the Heart: This video illustrates the importance of employee recognition and presents examples of the types of rewards leaders can give to truly motivate top performance.

Credibility: This two-part video series explores the difference between a person in a leadership position, and a person whose direction you are willing to follow.

The Credibility Factor: This program explores the relationship between leaders and their followers, and details the ingredients necessary for quality leadership.

To learn more, visit www.crmlearning.com or call 800-421-0833.